SkillBuilder

Grade 3

Math Workbook - 3

▸ *Measurement and Data*
▸ *Geometry*

Important Instruction

Students, Parents, and Teachers can use the URL or QR code provided below to access additional practice questions, educational videos, worksheets, mobile apps, standards information and more.

URL	QR Code
Visit the URL below and place the book access code **http://www.lumoslearning.com/a/tedbooks** **Access Code: SBMRG3M-95760-P**	

lumos learning
Developed by Expert Teachers

Contributing Author - Keyana M. Martinez
Contributing Author - LaSina McLain-Jackson
Executive Producer - Mukunda Krishnaswamy
Designer - Mirona Jova
Database Administrator - R. Raghavendra Rao

First Edition-2020

ISBN-10: 1-945730-04-8

ISBN-13: 978-1-945730-04-7

Printed in the United States of America

For permissions and additional information contact us

Lumos Information Services, LLC
Email: support@lumoslearning.com

PO Box 1575
Piscataway, NJ 08855-1575
Tel: (732) 384-0146
Fax: (866) 283-6471

http://www.LumosLearning.com

Lumos Measurement, Representation, Interpretation and Geometry Skill Builder, Grade 3 - Time, Liquid Volume & Mass and 2-Dimensional Shapes

This Book Includes:

- Practice questions to help students master
    - Measurement and Data
    - Geometry
- Detailed Answer explanations for every question
- Strategies for building speed and accuracy

Plus access to Online Workbooks which include:

- Instructional videos
- Mobile apps related to the learning objective
- Hundreds of additional practice questions
- Self-paced learning and personalized score reports
- Instant feedback after completion of the workbook

Lumos Learning
Developed by Expert Teachers

Table of Contents

Online Program Benefits

Students*

- Rigorous Standards Practice
- Technology-enhanced item types practice
- Additional learning resources such as videos and apps

Parents*

- You can review your student's online work by login to your parent account
- Pinpoint student areas of difficulty
- Develop custom lessons & assignments
- Access to High-Quality Question Bank

Teachers*

- Review the online work of your students
- Get insightful student reports
- Discover standards aligned videos, apps and books through EdSearch
- Easily access standards information along with the Coherence Map
- Create and share information about your classroom or school events

* Terms and Conditions apply

URL	QR Code
Visit the URL below and place the book access code **http://www.lumoslearning.com/a/tedbooks** **Access Code: SBMRG3M-95760-P**	

Start using the online resources included with this book today!

Introduction

Books in the Lumos Skill Builder series are designed to help students master specific skills in Math and English Language Arts. The content of each workbook is rigorous and aligned with the robust standards. Each standard, and substandard, has its own specific content. Taking the time to study and practice each standard individually can help students more adequately understand and demonstrate proficiency of that standard in their particular grade level.

Unlike traditional printed books, this book provides online access to engaging educational videos, mobile apps and assessments. Blending printed resources with technology based learning tools and resources has proven to be an effective strategy to help students of the current generation master learning objectives. We call these books tedBooks™ since they connect printed books to a repository of online learning resources!

Additionally, students have individual strengths and weaknesses. Being able to practice content by standard allows them the ability to more deeply understand each standard and be able to work to strengthen academic weaknesses. The online resources create personalized learning opportunities for each student and provides immediate individualized feedback.

We believe that yearlong learning and adequate practice before the test are the keys to success on standardized tests. The books in the Skill Builder series will help students gain foundational skills needed to perform well on the standardized tests.

How to Use this Book Effectively

The Lumos Program is a flexible learning tool. It can be adapted to suit a student's skill level and the time available to practice. Here are some tips to help you use this book and the online resources effectively:

Students

- The standards in each book can be practiced in the order designed, or in the order of your own choosing.
- Complete all problems in each workbook.
- Use the online workbooks to further practice your areas of difficulty and complement classroom learning.
- Watch videos recommended for the lesson or question.
- Download and try mobile apps related to what you are learning.

Parents

- Get student reports and useful information about your school by downloading the Lumos SchoolUp™ app. Please follow directions provided in "How to download Lumos SchoolUp™ App" section of this chapter.
- Review your child's performance in the "Lumos Online Workbooks" periodically. You can do this by simply asking your child to log into the system online and selecting the subject area you wish to review.
- Review your child's work in each workbook.

Measurement & Data

Telling Time

1. **What time does this clock show?**

   Ⓐ 3:12
   Ⓑ 2:17
   Ⓒ 2:22
   Ⓓ 2:03

2. **What time does this clock show?**

   Ⓐ 5:42
   Ⓑ 9:28
   Ⓒ 6:47
   Ⓓ 5:47

3. **What time does this clock show?**

   Ⓐ 10:00
   Ⓑ 12:50
   Ⓒ 10:02
   Ⓓ 9:41

4. **What time does this clock show?**

Ⓐ 12:39
Ⓑ 8:04
Ⓒ 1:38
Ⓓ 12:42

5. **On an analog clock, the shorter hand shows the _____ .**

Ⓐ minutes
Ⓑ hours
Ⓒ seconds
Ⓓ days

6. **On an analog clock, the longer hand shows the _____ .**

Ⓐ minutes
Ⓑ hours
Ⓒ days
Ⓓ seconds

7. **The clock currently shows:**

What time will it be in 8 minutes?

Ⓐ 1:38
Ⓑ 10:15
Ⓒ 10:10
Ⓓ 12:58

8. **The clock currently shows:**

   What time will it be in 20 minutes?

   Ⓐ 12:59
   Ⓑ 1:09
   Ⓒ 2:00
   Ⓓ 8:24

9. **The clock says:**

   What time was it 10 minutes ago?

   Ⓐ 1:29
   Ⓑ 12:29
   Ⓒ 12:49
   Ⓓ 1:09

10. **Lucy started her test at 12:09 PM and finished at 12:58 PM. David started at 12:15 PM and ended at 1:03 PM. Who finished in a shorter amount of time?**

    Ⓐ Lucy
    Ⓑ David
    Ⓒ They both took the same amount of time.
    Ⓓ There is not enough information given.

11. **The Jamisons are on a road trip that will take 5 hours and 25 minutes. They have been driving for 3 hours and 41 minutes. How much longer do they need to travel before they reach their destination?**

    Ⓐ 1 hour, 13 minutes
    Ⓑ 2 hours, 19 minutes
    Ⓒ 1 hour, 44 minutes
    Ⓓ 2 hours, 7 minutes

12. Rachel usually gets around 9 hours of sleep per night. She went to bed at 9:30 PM. About what time will she wake up?

Ⓐ 8:30 AM
Ⓑ 10:30 AM
Ⓒ 6:30 AM
Ⓓ 5:30 AM

13. A 45 minute long show ends at 12:20 PM. When did the show begin?

Ⓐ 1:05 PM
Ⓑ 11:35 AM
Ⓒ 11:35 PM
Ⓓ 11:45 AM

14. Mrs. James is giving her class a math test. She is allowing the students 40 minutes to finish the test. The test began at 10:22 AM. By what time must the students be finished?

Ⓐ 10:42 AM
Ⓑ 10:57 AM
Ⓒ 11:02 AM
Ⓓ 12:02 PM

15. The directions on a frozen pizza say to cook it for 25 minutes. Mr. Adams puts the frozen pizza in the oven at 5:43 PM. When will the pizza be done?

Ⓐ 6:08 PM
Ⓑ 6:18 PM
Ⓒ 6:13 PM
Ⓓ 5:58 PM

16. Which statements are true? Select all the correct answers.

Ⓐ The minute hand points to 4
Ⓑ The minute hand points to 6
Ⓒ The hour hand points to 6
Ⓓ The clock shows the time as 5:30

17. What time does this clock show? Write your answer in the box below.

```

```

18. Circle the clock that shows the time as 12:15

A   B   C

19. John starts working in the garden at 5:30 PM and finishes 40 minutes later. What time does the clock show when John finishes his work? Represent this on a number line.

```

```

20. **The clocks in the first column show different times. For each clock in the first column, select the correct answer.**

	9:42	11:58	2:03
	◯	◯	◯
	◯	◯	◯
	◯	◯	◯

Online Resources: Telling Time

URL	QR Code
http://lumoslearning.com/a/m13438	

 Videos   Apps   Sample Questions

NOTES

Elapsed Time

1. Cedric began reading his book at 9:12 AM. He finished at 10:02 AM. How long did it take him to read his book?

    Ⓐ 50 minutes
    Ⓑ 40 minutes
    Ⓒ 48 minutes
    Ⓓ 30 minutes

2. Samantha began eating her dinner at 7:11 PM and finished at 7:35 PM so that she could go to her room and play. How long did Samantha take to eat her dinner?

    Ⓐ 34 minutes
    Ⓑ 21 minutes
    Ⓒ 24 minutes
    Ⓓ 30 minutes

3. Tanya has after school tutoring from 3:00 PM until 3:25 PM. She began walking home at 3:31 PM and arrived at her house at 3:56 PM. How long did it take Tanya to walk home?

    Ⓐ 31 minutes
    Ⓑ 15 minutes
    Ⓒ 56 minutes
    Ⓓ 25 minutes

4. Doug loves to play video games. He started playing at 4:00 PM and did not finish until 5:27 PM. How long did Doug play video games?

    Ⓐ 1 hour and 37 minutes
    Ⓑ 1 hour and 27 minutes
    Ⓒ 27 minutes
    Ⓓ 2 hours and 27 minutes

5. Kelly has to clean her room before going to bed. She began cleaning her room at 6:12 PM. When she finished, it was 7:15 PM. How long did it take Kelly to clean her room?

    Ⓐ 57 minutes
    Ⓑ 53 minutes
    Ⓒ 1 hour and 3 minutes
    Ⓓ 1 hour and 15 minutes

6. Holly had a busy day. She attended a play from 7:06 PM until 8:13 PM. Then she went to dinner from 8:30 to 9:30 PM. How long did Holly attend the play?

   Ⓐ 57 minutes
   Ⓑ 2 hours and 27 minutes
   Ⓒ 46 minutes
   Ⓓ 1 hour and 7 minutes

7. Cara took her little brother to the park. They arrived at 3:11 PM and played until 4:37 PM. How long did Cara and her brother play at the park?

   Ⓐ 26 minutes
   Ⓑ 1 hour and 26 minutes
   Ⓒ 56 minutes
   Ⓓ 1 hour and 37 minutes

8. Arthur ran 5 miles. He began running at 8:19 AM and finished at 9:03 AM. How long did it take Arthur to run 5 miles?

   Ⓐ 44 minutes
   Ⓑ 45 minutes
   Ⓒ 40 minutes
   Ⓓ 54 minutes

9. Mr. Daniels wanted to see how fast he could wash the dishes. He began washing at 4:17 PM and finished at 4:32 PM. How long did it take Mr. Daniels to wash the dishes?

   Ⓐ 15 minutes
   Ⓑ 25 minutes
   Ⓒ 27 minutes
   Ⓓ 32 minutes

10. Sophia took a test that started at 3:28 PM. She finished the test at 4:11 PM. How long did it take Sophia to take her test?

   Ⓐ 37 minutes
   Ⓑ 47 minutes
   Ⓒ 33 minutes
   Ⓓ 43 minutes

11. Jonathan loves riding his bike, but he has to leave for football practice at 1:30 PM. If it is 1:11 PM now, how long does Jonathan have left to ride his bike before he has to leave for practice?

Ⓐ 9 minutes
Ⓑ 19 minutes
Ⓒ 21 minutes
Ⓓ 29 minutes

12. Mrs. Roberts loves to take a 20 minute nap on Saturdays. She was really tired when she went to sleep at 10:45 AM. She did not wake up until 11:25 AM. How long was Mrs. Roberts' long nap?

Ⓐ 40 minutes
Ⓑ 20 minutes
Ⓒ 60 minutes
Ⓓ 30 minutes

13. Spencer has to be at his piano lesson at noon. If it is now 11:29 AM, how long does Spencer have to get to his lesson?

Ⓐ 31 minutes
Ⓑ 1 minute
Ⓒ 29 minutes
Ⓓ 39 minutes

14. Look at the clocks below. How much time has elapsed between Clock A to Clock B?

Clock A	Clock B

Ⓐ 1 hour and 2 minutes
Ⓑ 1 hour and 12 minutes
Ⓒ 52 minutes
Ⓓ 42 minutes

15. Look at the clocks below. How much time has elapsed between Clock A to Clock B?

Clock A   Clock B

Ⓐ **52 minutes**
Ⓑ **42 minutes**
Ⓒ **12 minutes**
Ⓓ **32 minutes**

16. Tiana's daily schedule consists of classes that are 45 minutes long. The table shows what time some of her classes start. What time will each class end? Select the correct answer.

	9:05	10:55	12:15
History 10:10	○	○	○
Math 8:20	○	○	○
Gym 11:30	○	○	○

17. Jonas is taking a long road trip. He drives for one hour and then stops and rests for 15 minutes. He repeats this until the end of the trip. Complete the table to show his schedule.

Driving Start Time	Break Time
1:00	2:00
2:15	
3:30	4:30

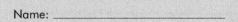
18. How much time has passed? Select all the correct answers.

Ⓐ 1 hour
Ⓑ 90 minutes
Ⓒ 2 hours
Ⓓ 120 minutes

19. Observe the two clocks. How many minutes have passed between the time shown in the first clock to the time in the second clock. Write your answer in the box given below.

20. Tim went out to do some work. He left home at 11:30 AM and returned back at 3:45 PM. How long was he away from home? Circle the correct answer.

Ⓐ 3 hours and 15 minutes
Ⓑ 4 hours and 15 minutes
Ⓒ 3 hours and 45 minutes
Ⓓ 4 hours and 45 minutes

20. Tim went out to do some work. He left home at 11:30 AM and returned back at 3:45 PM. How long was he away from home? Circle the correct answer.

Ⓐ 3 hours and 15 minutes
Ⓑ 4 hours and 15 minutes
Ⓒ 3 hours and 45 minutes
Ⓓ 4 hours and 45 minutes

Online Resources: Elapsed Time

URL	QR Code
http://lumoslearning.com/a/m13439	

 Videos   Apps   Sample Questions

NOTES

Liquid Volume & Mass

1. "40 pounds" is printed at the bottom of a bag of sand. The number "40" is being used to _____ .

   Ⓐ count
   Ⓑ name
   Ⓒ locate
   Ⓓ measure

2. In the metric system, which is the best unit to measure the mass of a coffee table?

   Ⓐ Milliliters
   Ⓑ Kilograms
   Ⓒ Grams
   Ⓓ Liters

3. Which unit should be used to measure the amount of water in a small bowl?

   Ⓐ Cups
   Ⓑ Gallons
   Ⓒ Inches
   Ⓓ Tons

4. Which unit in the customary system is best suited to measure the weight of a coffee table?

   Ⓐ Gallons
   Ⓑ Pounds
   Ⓒ Quarts
   Ⓓ Ounces

5. Which of these units could be used to measure the capacity of a container?

   Ⓐ pints
   Ⓑ feet
   Ⓒ pounds
   Ⓓ millimeters

6. Which of these is a unit of mass?

   Ⓐ liter
   Ⓑ meter
   Ⓒ gram
   Ⓓ degree

7. Which of these units has the greatest capacity?

    Ⓐ gallon
    Ⓑ pint
    Ⓒ cup
    Ⓓ quart

8. Which of these might be the weight of an average sized 8 year-old child?

    Ⓐ 15 pounds
    Ⓑ 30 pounds
    Ⓒ 65 pounds
    Ⓓ 150 pounds

9. Volume is measured in _____ units.

    Ⓐ cubic
    Ⓑ liters
    Ⓒ square
    Ⓓ box

10. What is an appropriate unit to measure the weight of a dog?

    Ⓐ tons
    Ⓑ pounds
    Ⓒ inches
    Ⓓ gallons

11. What is an appropriate unit to measure the amount of water in a swimming pool?

    Ⓐ teaspoons
    Ⓑ cups
    Ⓒ gallons
    Ⓓ inches

12. What is an appropriate unit to measure the distance across a city?

    Ⓐ centimeters
    Ⓑ feet
    Ⓒ inches
    Ⓓ miles

13. What is an appropriate unit to measure the amount of salt in a cupcake recipe?

   Ⓐ teaspoons
   Ⓑ gallons
   Ⓒ miles
   Ⓓ kilograms

14. Which unit is the largest?

   Ⓐ mile
   Ⓑ centimeter
   Ⓒ foot
   Ⓓ inch

15. Which unit is the smallest?

   Ⓐ kilometer
   Ⓑ centimeter
   Ⓒ millimeter
   Ⓓ inch

16. Which units of measurement could be used to measure how much water a pot can hold? Select all the correct answers.

   Ⓐ quarts
   Ⓑ centimeter
   Ⓒ liters
   Ⓓ miles

17. Observe the figure given. How many cups of liquid does this measuring cup hold? Write your answer in the box given below.

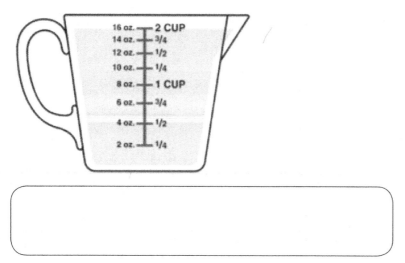

18. Circle the tool that should be used to measure a small amount of sugar.

19. There are 8 water coolers in a school. Each water cooler holds 7 liters of water. All the water coolers were filled up in the morning. In the evening 5 liters of water remained. How much water was consumed? Explain how you got the answer in the box below.

Online Resources: Liquid, Volume & Mass

URL	QR Code
http://lumoslearning.com/a/m13440	

 Videos   Apps   Sample Questions

NOTES

Graphs

1.

Class Survey Should there be a field trip?		
	Yes	**No**
Mr. A's class	⊥⊥⊤⊤ ⊥⊥⊤⊤ ||||	⊥⊥⊤⊤ ||
Mr. B's class	⊥⊥⊤⊤ ⊥⊥⊤⊤ ⊥⊥⊤⊤	⊥⊥⊤⊤ ⊥⊥⊤⊤ |||
Mr. C's class	⊥⊥⊤⊤ ⊥⊥⊤⊤ |	⊥⊥⊤⊤ ⊥⊥⊤⊤ |
Mr. D's class	⊥⊥⊤⊤ ⊥⊥⊤⊤ ||	⊥⊥⊤⊤ ⊥⊥⊤⊤

Four 3rd grade classes in Hill Elementary School were surveyed to find out if they wanted to go on a field trip at the end of the school year. The tally table above was used to record the votes.

How many kids voted "Yes" in Mrs. B's class?

Ⓐ 28 kids
Ⓑ 15 kids
Ⓒ 13 kids
Ⓓ 23 kids

2.

Should there be a field trip?		
	Yes	No
Mr. A's class	14	7
Mr. B's class	15	13
Mr. C's class	11	11
Mr. D's class	12	10
Total	52	41

Four 3rd grade classes in Hill Elementary School were surveyed to find out if they wanted to go on a field trip at the end of the school year. The table above shows the results of the survey.

How many kids voted "Yes" in Mr. A's class?

Ⓐ 7 kids
Ⓑ 15 kids
Ⓒ 14 kids
Ⓓ 21 kids

3.

Should there be a field trip?		
	Yes	No
Mr. A's class	14	7
Mr. B's class	15	13
Mr. C's class	11	11
Mr. D's class	12	10
Total	52	41

Four 3rd grade classes in Hill Elementary School were surveyed to find out if they wanted to go on a field trip at the end of the school year. The table above shows the results of the survey.

How many kids altogether voted "No" for the field trip?

Ⓐ 82 kids
Ⓑ 11 kids
Ⓒ 52 kids
Ⓓ 41 kids

4. The students in Mr. Donovan's class were surveyed to find out their favorite school subjects. The results are shown in the pictograph. Use the pictograph to answer the following question:

How many students chose either science or math?

Our Favorite Subjects

Math	○ ○ ○ ○
Reading	○ ○
Science	○ ○ ○
History	○
Other	○ ○

Key: ○ = 2 votes

Ⓐ 6 students
Ⓑ 7 students
Ⓒ 14 students
Ⓓ 2 students

5.

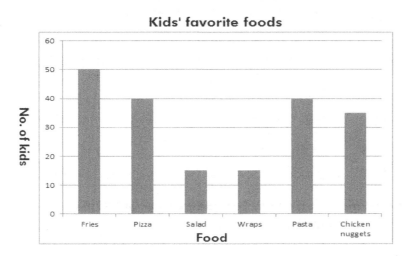

The third graders in Valley Elementary School were asked to pick their favorite food from 6 choices. The results are shown in the bar graph.
Which food was the favorite of the most children?

Ⓐ Pizza
Ⓑ Pasta
Ⓒ Fries
Ⓓ Salad

6.

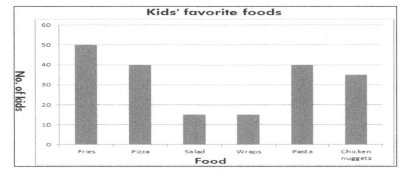

The third graders in Valley Elementary School were asked to pick their favorite food from 6 choices. The results are shown in the bar graph.

What are the 2 foods that kids like the least?

Ⓐ Fries and Pizza
Ⓑ Pizza and Pasta
Ⓒ Pasta and Chicken Nuggets
Ⓓ Salad and Wraps

7.

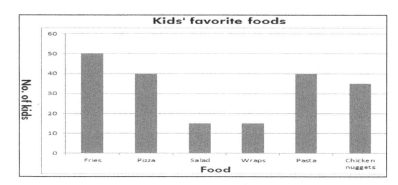

The third graders in Valley Elementary School were asked to pick their favorite food from 6 choices. The results are shown in the bar graph.

How many kids chose pasta?

Ⓐ 50 kids
Ⓑ 15 kids
Ⓒ 40 kids
Ⓓ 35 kids

8.

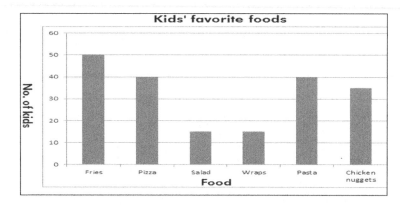

The third graders in Valley Elementary School were asked to pick their favorite food from 6 choices. The results are shown in the bar graph.

How many more kids prefer fries than pizza?

Ⓐ 50 more kids
Ⓑ 10 more kids
Ⓒ 1 more kid
Ⓓ 15 more kids

9.

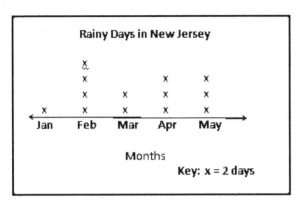

The line plot shows the number of days it rained in New Jersey from January through May. What is the title of the above graph?

Ⓐ Line plot
Ⓑ Rainy Days in New Jersey
Ⓒ Months
Ⓓ 2 days

10.

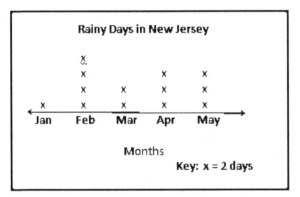

Which of the following statements about the above graph is true?

Ⓐ The graph shows the amount of rain accumulated each day.
Ⓑ The graph shows New Jersey's monthly rainy days from January through May.
Ⓒ The graph shows the average temperature during the 5 month period.
Ⓓ The graph shows New Jersey's total number of rainy days for the year.

11.

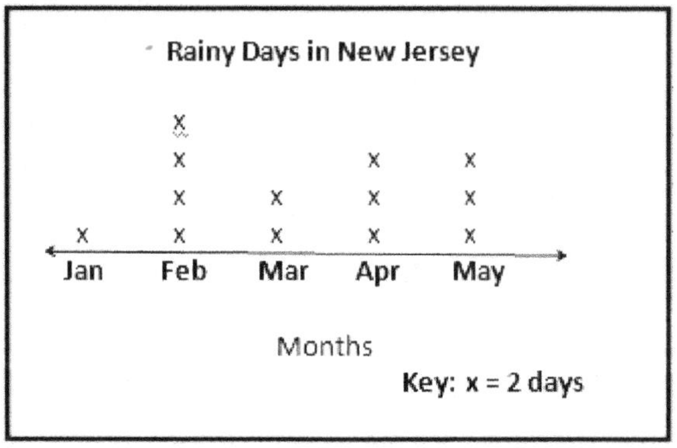

Rainy Days in New Jersey

```
        X
        X           X       X
        X   X       X       X
    X   X   X       X       X
    Jan Feb Mar    Apr     May
```

Months

Key: x = 2 days

According to the graph, which month had the most of rainy days?

Ⓐ March
Ⓑ February
Ⓒ January
Ⓓ April

12. A survey was taken to find out the favorite sports of third graders in a particular class. The results are shown in the tally table. Use the table to answer the following question:

How many students were surveyed altogether?

Our Favorite Sports

Soccer	ℕ| |
Tennis	||||
Baseball	ℕ| |||
Hockey	||||
Other	|||

Ⓐ 20 students
Ⓑ 25 students
Ⓒ 24 students
Ⓓ 27 students

13. **A survey was taken to find out the favorite sports of third graders in a particular class. The results are shown in the tally table. Use the table to answer the following question:**

    How many more students chose soccer than chose hockey?

    Our Favorite Sports

Soccer	⊬Ⅱ Ⅰ
Tennis	Ⅰ Ⅰ Ⅰ Ⅰ
Baseball	⊬Ⅱ Ⅰ Ⅰ Ⅰ
Hockey	Ⅰ Ⅰ Ⅰ Ⅰ
Other	Ⅰ Ⅰ Ⅰ

    Ⓐ 6 students
    Ⓑ 4 students
    Ⓒ 2 students
    Ⓓ 3 students

14. **A survey was taken to find out the favorite sports of third graders in a particular class. The results are shown in the tally table. Use the table to answer the following question:**

    How many students chose baseball as their favorite sport?

    Our Favorite Sports

Soccer	⊬Ⅱ Ⅰ
Tennis	Ⅰ Ⅰ Ⅰ Ⅰ
Baseball	⊬Ⅱ Ⅰ Ⅰ Ⅰ
Hockey	Ⅰ Ⅰ Ⅰ Ⅰ
Other	Ⅰ Ⅰ Ⅰ

    Ⓐ 9 students
    Ⓑ 8 students
    Ⓒ 3 students
    Ⓓ 6 students

15. A survey was taken to find out the favorite sports of third graders in a particular class. The results are shown in the tally table. Use the table to answer the following question: Which two sports were chosen by the same number of students?

Our Favorite Sports

Soccer	𝍶𝍶 I
Tennis	IIII
Baseball	𝍶𝍶 III
Hockey	IIII
Other	III

Ⓐ soccer and tennis
Ⓑ soccer and baseball
Ⓒ hockey and soccer
Ⓓ hockey and tennis

16. Mrs. Brown's class voted on which day they will have a class party. Look at the graph. Each figure represents 1 student. Match the correct answers to the number of votes.

Student Party Day Votes

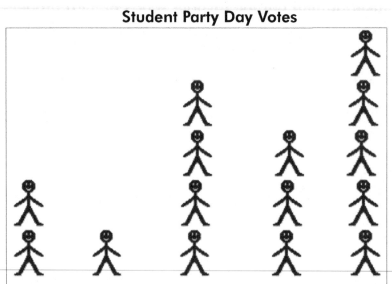

Monday   Tuesday   Wednesday   Thursday   Friday

	5	2	4
Total votes for Friday	○	○	○
Total votes for Wednesday	○	○	○
Total votes for Monday	○	○	○

17. Coach Dennis is creating a graph. He wants to purchase bats for his team. He needs to purchase 8 bats. He needs half of the bats to be made of wood. The other half will be made of aluminum. He decides that he will purchase 3 more bats made of plastic as well. Complete the table by filling in the correct answers.

Type of Bat	Number of Bats Needed
Wood	
Aluminum	
Plastic	

18. Vicki is planting a flower garden. The graph above shows the amount of flowers to be planted in the garden. Which of the following statements are true? Select all the correct answers.

 = 2 Hibiscus flowers

 = 2 Rose flowers

 = 2 Iris flowers

Ⓐ
Ⓑ The count of Rose flowers is 14
Ⓒ The Count of Rose flowers is 7
Ⓓ The count of Hibiscus flowers is 4
     The count of Iris flowers is 6

19. Find the total number of each coin. Use the tally chart to draw a bar graph.

Coins in John's Piggy Bank		
Coin	Tally	Number of Coins
Penny	ⅢⅢ ⅢⅢ ⅢⅢ ⅢⅢ II	
Nickel	ⅢⅢ ⅢⅢ ⅢⅢ III	
Dime	ⅢⅢ ⅢⅢ IIII	
Quarter	ⅢⅢ ⅢⅢ ⅢⅢ I	

20. From the Venn Diagram given below, represent the number of people who only own cats as pet to the number of people who own only dogs as a pet in the form of a fraction $\frac{a}{b}$ (ratio of number of people owning cats to dogs)

Pets We Have

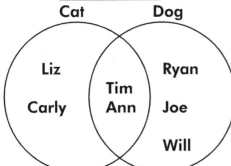

Online Resources: Graphs

URL	QR Code
http://lumoslearning.com/a/m13441	

 Videos   Apps   Sample Questions

NOTES

Measuring Length

1. Which of these units is part of the metric system?

    Ⓐ Foot
    Ⓑ Mile
    Ⓒ Kilometer
    Ⓓ Yard

2. Which metric unit is closest in length to one yard?

    Ⓐ decimeter
    Ⓑ meter
    Ⓒ millimeter
    Ⓓ kilometer

3. Which of these is the best estimate for the length of a table?

    Ⓐ 2 decimeters
    Ⓑ 2 centimeters
    Ⓒ 2 meters
    Ⓓ 2 kilometers

4. What unit should you use to measure the length of a book?

    Ⓐ Kilometers
    Ⓑ Meters
    Ⓒ Centimeters
    Ⓓ Grams

5. About how long is a new pencil?

    Ⓐ 8 inches
    Ⓑ 8 feet
    Ⓒ 8 yards
    Ⓓ 8 miles

6. Which of these is the best estimate for the length of a football?

  Ⓐ 1 foot
  Ⓑ 2 feet
  Ⓒ 6 feet
  Ⓓ 4 feet

7. Complete the following statement.
   The length of a football field is _____.

  Ⓐ less than one meter
  Ⓑ greater than one meter
  Ⓒ about one meter
  Ⓓ impossible to measure

8. Complete the following statement.
   An adult's pointer finger is about one _____ wide.

  Ⓐ meter
  Ⓑ kilometer
  Ⓒ millimeter
  Ⓓ centimeter

9. Complete the following statement.
   The distance between two cities would most likely be measured in _____.

  Ⓐ hours
  Ⓑ miles
  Ⓒ yards
  Ⓓ square inches

10. A ribbon is 25 centimeters long. About how many inches long is it?

  Ⓐ 2
  Ⓑ 25
  Ⓒ 10
  Ⓓ 50

11.

How long is this object?

Ⓐ 4 inches
Ⓑ 8 inches
Ⓒ 10 inches
Ⓓ 12 inches

12.

How long is this object?

Ⓐ 2 inches
Ⓑ 5 inches
Ⓒ 3 inches
Ⓓ 1 inch

13.

How long is this object?

Ⓐ 6 inches
Ⓑ 5 and a half inches
Ⓒ 6 and a half inches
Ⓓ 7 inches

14. Which statement is correct?

Ⓐ 1 inch > 1 mile
Ⓑ 1 inch > 1 centimeter
Ⓒ 1 foot < 1 inch
Ⓓ 1 mile < 1 foot

17. Observe the figure. How long is the pencil when measured in inches?

18. Fill in the correct answer in the blanks shown in the table.

Measurement in inches	Measurement in half inches	Measurement in quarter inches
$3\frac{1}{2}$ inches	7 half inches	14 quarter inches
$2\frac{1}{2}$ inches		
	11 half inches	
		26 quarter inches

19. Use the line plot to answer the questions given in the first column.

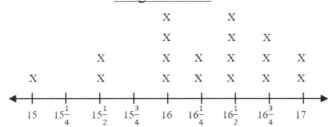

Lengths of Fish

Instruction:
X = 2 fishes

	4	6	8
How many fish are $16\frac{1}{2}$ inches long?	○	○	○
How many more fish are 16 inches long than 17 inches?	○	○	○
How many fish are less than $15\frac{3}{4}$ inches long?	○	○	○

Online Resources: Measuring Length

URL	QR Code
http://lumoslearning.com/a/m13442	

 Videos   Apps   Sample Questions

NOTES

Name: _____   Date: _____

Area

1. The area of a plane figure is measured in _____ units.

    Ⓐ cubic
    Ⓑ meter
    Ⓒ square
    Ⓓ box

2. Which of these objects has an area of about 1 square inch?

    Ⓐ a sheet of writing paper
    Ⓑ a beach towel
    Ⓒ a dollar bill
    Ⓓ a postage stamp

3. Mr. Parker wants to cover a mural with cloth. The mural is 12 inches long and 20 inches wide. How many square inches of cloth does Mr. Parker need?

    Ⓐ 240 square inches
    Ⓑ 32 square inches
    Ⓒ 120 square inches
    Ⓓ 220 square inches

4.

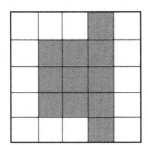

    ☐ = 1 Square Unit

    What is the area of the shaded region?

    Ⓐ 10 square units
    Ⓑ 8 square units
    Ⓒ 11 square units
    Ⓓ 15 square units

5. **Find the area of this figure.**

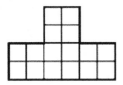

☐ = 1 Square Unit

Ⓐ **22 square units**
Ⓑ **20 square units**
Ⓒ **18 square units**
Ⓓ **16 square units**

6. **Find the area of this figure.**

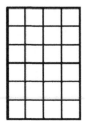

☐ = 1 Square Unit

Ⓐ **22 square units**
Ⓑ **20 square units**
Ⓒ **24 square units**
Ⓓ **28 square units**

7. **Find the area of the shaded region.**

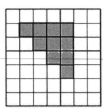

☐ = 1 Square Unit

Ⓐ **11 square units**
Ⓑ **10 square units**
Ⓒ **16 square units**
Ⓓ **9 square units**

8. Find the area of the shaded region.

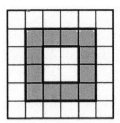

☐ = 1 Square Unit

Ⓐ 16 square units
Ⓑ 12 square units
Ⓒ 10 square units
Ⓓ 11 square units

9. Find the area of the shaded region.

Key: ☐ = 1 Square Unit

Ⓐ 5 square units
Ⓑ 6 square units
Ⓒ 8 square units
Ⓓ 9 square units

10. The area of Karen's rectangular room is 72 sq. ft. If the length of the room is 8 ft. What is its width? Drag your answer into the box. Find the area of the shaded region.

Ⓐ 8 ft.
Ⓑ 6 ft.
Ⓒ 7 ft.
Ⓓ 9 ft.

11. Can these items be measured in square units? Select yes or no.

	Yes	No
Window panes		
A ball		
Bathroom tile		
A banana		

12. Find the area of the shaded region in each figure. Each box is 1 square unit. Write your answers in the blank boxes in the table.

Figure A

Figure B

Figure C

Figure	Area
Figure A	
Figure B	
Figure C	

13. Find the area of the figure. Write your answer in the box given below.

6 feet

9 feet

square feet

14. Which of the following are possible ways to find the area of this figure? Each box is 1 square unit. Select all correct answers.

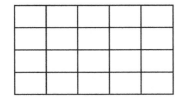

Ⓐ Count the total number of square units
Ⓑ Multiplying the length by the width of the figure
Ⓒ Multiplying the number of square units by 2
Ⓓ Subtracting the length of the figure from the width

15. The area of a rectangle A is 75 sq. cm. The area of square B is one third the area of the rectangle A. What is the side length of the square B? Circle the correct answer.

Ⓐ 7 cm
Ⓑ 5 cm
Ⓒ 4 cm
Ⓓ 6 cm

Online Resources: Area

URL	QR Code

http://lumoslearning.com/a/m13443

 Videos   Apps   📖 Sample Questions

NOTES

Relating Area to Addition & Multiplication

1. **Find the area of the object below.**

3 feet

29 feet

Ⓐ 87 square feet
Ⓑ 32 square feet
Ⓒ 64 square feet
Ⓓ 128 square feet

2. **Find the area of the object below.**

12 yards

15 yards

Ⓐ 108 square yards
Ⓑ 54 square yards
Ⓒ 27 square yards
Ⓓ 180 square yards

3. **How could the area of this figure be calculated?**

33 inches

63 inches

Ⓐ Multiply 63 x 33 x 63 x 33
Ⓑ Add 63 + 33 + 63 + 33
Ⓒ Multiply 63 x 33
Ⓓ Multiply 2 x 63 x 33

4. **Find the area of the object below.**

5 meters

10 meters

   Ⓐ 75 square meters
   Ⓑ 50 square meters
   Ⓒ 15 square meters
   Ⓓ 30 square meters

5. **Find the area of the object below.**

16 yards

11 yards

   Ⓐ 176 square yards
   Ⓑ 27 square yards
   Ⓒ 54 square yards
   Ⓓ 2,916 square yards

6. **Find the area of the object below.**

3 inches

2 inches + 3 inches

   Ⓐ 18 square inches
   Ⓑ 15 square inches
   Ⓒ 9 square inches
   Ⓓ 6 square inches

7. **Find the area of the object below.**

7 feet

2 feet + 1 foot

   Ⓐ 16 square feet
   Ⓑ 14 square feet
   Ⓒ 9 square feet
   Ⓓ 21 square feet

8. Find the area of the object below.

12 meters

4 meters + 3 meters

  Ⓐ 84 square meters
  Ⓑ 48 square meters
  Ⓒ 36 square meters
  Ⓓ 72 square meters

9. Find the area of the object below.

5 inches

5 inches + 2 inches

  Ⓐ 12 square inches
  Ⓑ 10 square inches
  Ⓒ 25 square inches
  Ⓓ 35 square inches

10. Find the area of the object below.

13 yards

7 yards+7 yards

  Ⓐ 84 square yards
  Ⓑ 182 square yards
  Ⓒ 26 square yards
  Ⓓ 19 square yards

11. The city wants to plant grass in a park. The park is 20 feet by 50 feet. How much grass
    will they need to cover the entire park?

  Ⓐ 100 square feet
  Ⓑ 500 square feet
  Ⓒ 1,000 square feet
  Ⓓ 1,100 square feet

12. Brenda wants to purchase a rug for her room. Her room is a rectangle that measures 7 yards by 6 yards. What is the area of her room?

Ⓐ 42 square yards
Ⓑ 48 square yards
Ⓒ 36 square yards
Ⓓ 26 square yards

13. Joan wants to cover her backyard with flowers. If her backyard is 30 feet long and 20 feet wide, what is the area that needs to be covered in flowers?

Ⓐ 60 square feet
Ⓑ 500 square feet
Ⓒ 600 square feet
Ⓓ 100 square feet

14. Bethany decided to paint the four walls in her room. If each wall measures 20 feet by 10 feet, how many total square feet will she need to paint?

Ⓐ 400 square feet
Ⓑ 200 square feet
Ⓒ 800 square feet
Ⓓ 600 square feet

15. Seth wants to cover his table top with a piece of fabric. His table is 2 meters long and 4 meters wide. How much fabric does Seth need?

Ⓐ 6 square meters
Ⓑ 10 square meters
Ⓒ 8 square meters
Ⓓ 16 square meters

Online Resources: Relating Area to Addition & Multiplication

URL	QR Code
http://lumoslearning.com/a/m15223	

 Videos   Apps   Sample Questions

NOTES

Perimeter

1. **What is meant by the "perimeter" of a shape?**

    Ⓐ The distance from the center of a plane figure to its edge
    Ⓑ The distance from one corner of a plane figure to an opposite corner
    Ⓒ The distance around the outside of a plane figure
    Ⓓ The amount of space covered by a plane figure

2. **Complete the following statement.**
    Two measurements associated with plane figures are _____.

    Ⓐ perimeter and volume
    Ⓑ perimeter and area
    Ⓒ volume and area
    Ⓓ weight and volume

3.

    This rectangle is 4 units long and one unit wide. What is its perimeter?

    Ⓐ 10 units
    Ⓑ 4 units
    Ⓒ 5 units
    Ⓓ 8 units

4.

    2 units

    1 unit

    What is the perimeter of the rectangle?

    Ⓐ 5 units
    Ⓑ 6 units
    Ⓒ 3 units
    Ⓓ 2 units

5.

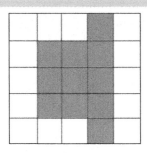

= 1 Square Unit

What is the perimeter of the shaded region in the above figure?

Ⓐ 16 units
Ⓑ 15 units
Ⓒ 11 units
Ⓓ 10 units

6. **The perimeter of this rhombus is 20 units. How long is each of its sides?**

Ⓐ 4 units
Ⓑ 10 units
Ⓒ 5 units
Ⓓ This cannot be determined.

7. **Each side of this rhombus measures 3 centimeters. What is its perimeter?**

Ⓐ 3 centimeters
Ⓑ 12 centimeters
Ⓒ 9 centimeters
Ⓓ 6 centimeters

8. This square has a perimeter of 80 units. How long is each of its sides?

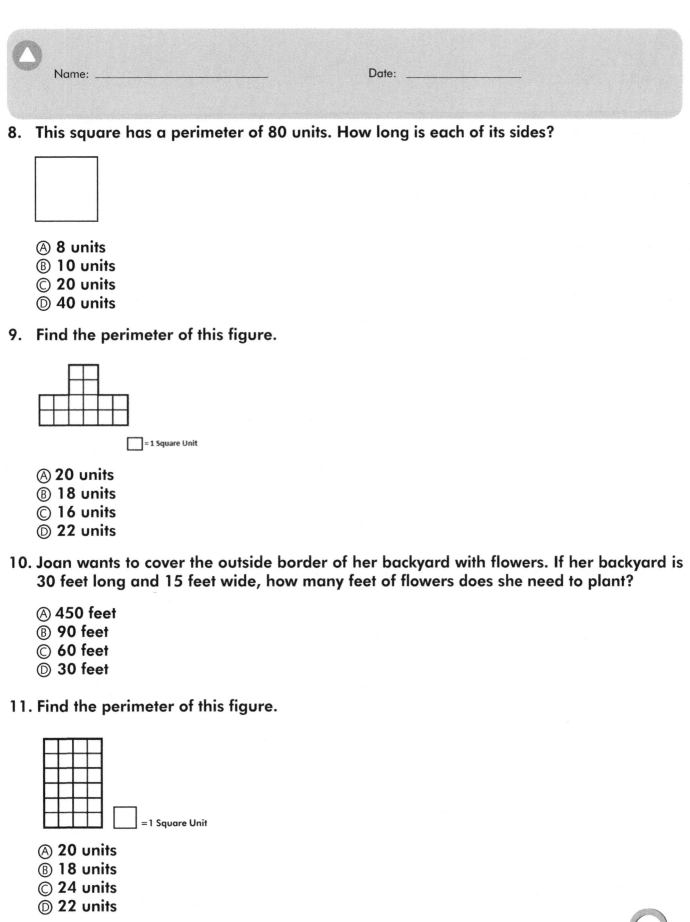

Ⓐ 8 units
Ⓑ 10 units
Ⓒ 20 units
Ⓓ 40 units

9. Find the perimeter of this figure.

= 1 Square Unit

Ⓐ 20 units
Ⓑ 18 units
Ⓒ 16 units
Ⓓ 22 units

10. Joan wants to cover the outside border of her backyard with flowers. If her backyard is 30 feet long and 15 feet wide, how many feet of flowers does she need to plant?

Ⓐ 450 feet
Ⓑ 90 feet
Ⓒ 60 feet
Ⓓ 30 feet

11. Find the perimeter of this figure.

=1 Square Unit

Ⓐ 20 units
Ⓑ 18 units
Ⓒ 24 units
Ⓓ 22 units

8. This square has a perimeter of 80 units. How long is each of its sides?

Ⓐ 8 units
Ⓑ 10 units
Ⓒ 20 units
Ⓓ 40 units

9. Find the perimeter of this figure.

☐ = 1 Square Unit

Ⓐ 20 units
Ⓑ 18 units
Ⓒ 16 units
Ⓓ 22 units

10. Joan wants to cover the outside border of her backyard with flowers. If her backyard is 30 feet long and 15 feet wide, how many feet of flowers does she need to plant?

Ⓐ 450 feet
Ⓑ 90 feet
Ⓒ 60 feet
Ⓓ 30 feet

11. Find the perimeter of this figure.

☐ = 1 Square Unit

Ⓐ 20 units
Ⓑ 18 units
Ⓒ 24 units
Ⓓ 22 units

12. Brenda wants to place rope around a large field in order to play a game. The field is a rectangle that measures 23 yards by 32 yards. How much rope does Brenda need?

Ⓐ 64 yards
Ⓑ 736 yards
Ⓒ 110 yards
Ⓓ 55 yards

13. Find the perimeter of the following object.

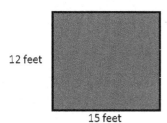

Ⓐ 54 feet
Ⓑ 27 feet
Ⓒ 58 feet
Ⓓ 180 feet

14. Find the perimeter of the following object.

Ⓐ 42 feet
Ⓑ 176 feet
Ⓒ 27 feet
Ⓓ 54 feet

15. Find the perimeter of the shaded region.

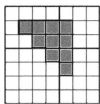

☐ = 1 Square Unit

Ⓐ 10 units
Ⓑ 13 units
Ⓒ 15 units
Ⓓ 16 units

16. Find the perimeter of the following object.

3 feet

29 feet

Ⓐ 32 feet
Ⓑ 87 feet
Ⓒ 172 feet
Ⓓ 64 feet

17. The city is building a fence around a park. The park is 20 feet by 50 feet. How many feet of fencing do they need?

20 feet

50 feet

Ⓐ 100 feet
Ⓑ 120 feet
Ⓒ 140 feet
Ⓓ 70 feet

18. Find the perimeter of the following object.

33 inches

53 inches

Ⓐ 86 inches
Ⓑ 172 inches
Ⓒ 1,749 inches
Ⓓ 50 inches

19. Find the perimeter of the following object.

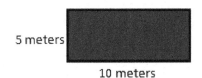

5 meters
10 meters

Ⓐ 15 meters
Ⓑ 25 meters
Ⓒ 30 meters
Ⓓ 50 meters

20. The perimeter of the following object is 16 feet. Find the length of the missing side.

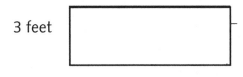

3 feet

x

Ⓐ x = 5 feet
Ⓑ x = 10 feet
Ⓒ x = 13 feet
Ⓓ x = 6 feet

21. The perimeter of the following object is 20 feet. Find the length of the missing side.

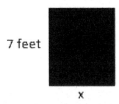

7 feet

x

Ⓐ x = 3 feet
Ⓑ x = 6 feet
Ⓒ x = 13 feet
Ⓓ x = 7 feet

22. The city is building a fence around a park. The park is 20 feet by 50 feet. If they only want the fence on 3 sides, what is the least amount of fencing they could buy?

Ⓐ 140 feet
Ⓑ 100 feet
Ⓒ 120 feet
Ⓓ 90 feet

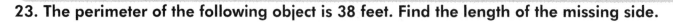

23. The perimeter of the following object is 38 feet. Find the length of the missing side.

12 feet

x

Ⓐ x = 17 feet
Ⓑ x = 12 feet
Ⓒ x = 7 feet
Ⓓ x = 26 feet

24. The perimeter of the following object is 24 inches. Find the length of the missing side.

5 inches

x

Ⓐ x = 19 inches
Ⓑ x = 7 inches
Ⓒ x = 9 inches
Ⓓ x = 12 inches

25. The perimeter of the following object is 54 yards. Find the length of the missing side.

13 yards

x

Ⓐ x = 28 yards
Ⓑ x = 14 yards
Ⓒ x = 41 yards
Ⓓ x = 27 yards

26. Which of the following statements are true? Select all correct answers.

Ⓐ The perimeter is the distance around the outside of a plane figure.
Ⓑ The perimeter is the center of a circle.
Ⓒ The perimeter can be found by adding the angles of a triangle.
Ⓓ The perimeter can be found by adding the length of a figure's sides.

27. What is the perimeter of the rectangle shown in figure below? Write your answer in the box given

3 units

6 units

28. Circle the rhombus that has a perimeter of 8.0 cm.

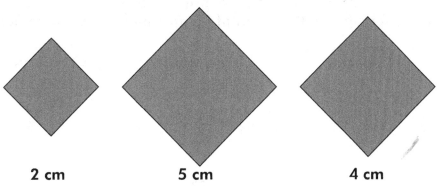

2 cm   5 cm   4 cm

29. John draws a regular hexagon. Each side measures 8 centimeters. He also draws a regular octagon. Each side of the octagon measures 7 centimeters. Which shape has a greater perimeter? How did you arrive at the answer?

30. The perimeters of the rectangles are given in the first column. For each perimeter, select the possible areas of the rectangles.
Note that for each perimeter, more than one option may be correct.
Instruction: Assume that the length and the width of the rectangles are whole numbers.

	15 sq. cm.	10 sq. cm.	12 sq. cm.
Perimeter = 16 cm	☐	☐	☐
Perimeter = 14 cm	☐	☐	☐
Perimeter = 22 cm	☐	☐	☐

30. The perimeters of the rectangles are given in the first column. For each perimeter, select the possible areas of the rectangles.

   Note that for each perimeter, more than one option may be correct.

   Instruction: Assume that the length and the width of the rectangles are whole numbers.

	15 sq. cm.	10 sq. cm.	12 sq. cm.
Perimeter = 16 cm	☐	☐	☐
Perimeter = 14 cm	☐	☐	☐
Perimeter = 22 cm	☐	☐	☐

Online Resources: Perimeter

URL	QR Code
http://lumoslearning.com/a/m13444	

 Videos   Apps   Sample Questions

End of Measurement & Data

NOTES

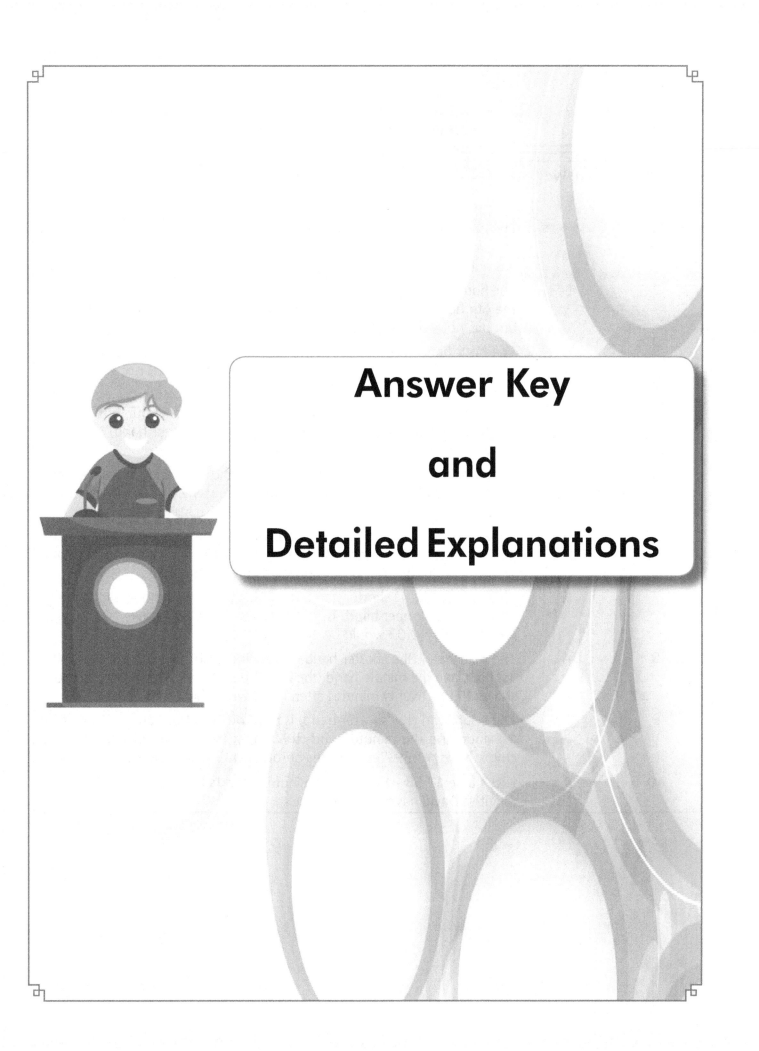

Answer Key

and

Detailed Explanations

Lesson 1: Telling Time

Question No.	Answer	Detailed Explanation
1	B	The hour hand (the shorter hand) is past the 2nd hour but has not reached the 3rd hour, and the minute hand (the longer hand) is past 15 minutes but has not yet reached 20 minutes.
2	D	The hour hand (the shorter hand) is past the 5th hour but has not reached the 6th hour, and the minute hand (the longer hand) is past 45 minutes but has not yet reached 50 minutes.
3	C	The hour hand (the shorter hand) is pointing to the 10th hour, and the minute hand (the longer hand) is past 0 minutes but has not yet reached 5 minutes.
4	A	The hour hand (the shorter hand) is past the 12th hour but has not reached the 1st hour, and the minute hand (the longer hand) is past 35 minutes but has not yet quite reached 40 minutes.
5	B	On a clock, the shorter hand points toward the hour and the longer hand points toward the minutes. For example, if it was 2:00, the shorter hand would point to the "2."
6	A	On a clock, the shorter hand points toward the hour and the longer hand points toward the minutes. For example, if it was 2:30, the longer hand would point to the "6," which represents the 30th minutes.
7	C	The hour hand (the shorter hand) is pointed at the 10th hour, and the minute hand (the longer hand) is at 2 minutes. The clock shows 10:02. Eight minutes after 10:02 would be 10:10.
8	A	The hour hand (the shorter hand) is past the 12th hour but not yet at the 1st hour, and the minute hand (the longer hand) is at 39 minutes. The clock shows 12:39. Twenty minutes after 12:39 would be 12:59.
9	B	The hour hand (the shorter hand) is past the 12th hour but not yet at the 1st hour, and the minute hand (the longer hand) is at 39 minutes. The clock shows 12:39. Ten minutes before 12:39 would be 12:29.
10	B.	Lucy's time:12:58 - 12:09 = 49 minutes. David's time: 1:03 - 12:15 = 48 minutes. David has the shorter time.

Question No.	Answer	Detailed Explanation
11	C	You can solve this problem by converting the hours to minutes and then subtracting the two times. 5 hours and 25 minutes is equivalent to (5 x 60) + 25 = 325 minutes. You multiply 5 hours by 60 because there are 60 minutes in an hour. 3 hours and 41 minutes is equivalent to (3 x 60) + 41 = 221 minutes. 325 - 221 = 104. Now convert 104 minutes back into hours and minutes by dividing by 60 and the answer is 1 hour and 44 minutes.
12	C	To calculate how many hours of sleep Rachel will receive, add the amount of time she sleeps to the time she goes to bed. 9 hours after 9:30 PM would be 6:30 AM.
13	B	To calculate when the show began, subtract the length of the show from the ending time. Counting back 45 minutes from 12:20 PM, you would arrive at 11:35 AM. The PM changes to AM, since you are now before noon.
14	C	To calculate when the students have to be finished with their test, add the amount of time given for the test to the start time. 40 minutes after 10:22 AM would be 11:02 AM.
15	A	To calculate when the pizza will be done, add the cooking time to the time Mr. Adams began cooking. 25 minutes after 5:43 PM would be 6:08 PM.
16	B & D	On an analog clock, the long hand shows the minutes while the short hand shows the hour. The minute hand on this clock points to 6 which represents 30 minutes. The hour hand is in between the numbers 5 and 6 which shows that the time is 5:30.
17	1:00	On an analog clock, the long hand shows the minutes while the short hand shows the hour. The minute hand on this clock points to 12 which represents an exact hour. The hour hand points to the number 1 shows that the time is exactly 1:00.
18	Clock A	Clock A is the correct answer. On an analog clock, the long hand shows the minutes while the short hand shows the hour. The minute hand on this clock points to 3 which represents 15 minutes. The hour hand is nearest to the number 12 which shows that the time is 12:15.

Question No.	Answer	Detailed Explanation

19

To determine what time John finishes his work, add 40 minutes to 5:30 PM; 5:30 PM + 40 minutes = 6:10 PM. This is represented on the number line below.

5:30		5:45			6:00		6:10	6:15		

In the figure, green dot shows the time when John started the work, and the red dot shows the time when John finished his work.

20

	9:42	11:58	2:03
	○	●	○
	○	○	●
	●	○	○

(1) In the first clock, the hour hand (the shorter hand) has passed the 11th hour but not yet at the 12th hour.
At the start of the hour, the minute hand (the longer hand) points directly to 12, and it takes 5 minutes to move from one number to the next number and one minute to move from one tick to the next tick. So, the minute hand is at 58 minutes (5 x 11 + 3 = 58).
Therefore, the clock shows 11:58.

(2) In the second clock, the hour hand (the shorter hand) has passed the 2nd hour but not yet at the 3rd hour.
The minute hand is at 3 minutes (1 x 3 = 3).
Therefore, the clock shows 2:03.

(3) In the third clock, the hour hand (the shorter hand) has passed the 9th hour but not yet at the 10th hour.
The minute hand is at 42 minutes (5 x 8 + 2 = 42).
Therefore, the clock shows 9:42.

Elapsed Time

Question No.	Answer	Detailed Explanation
1	A	Counting back from 10:02 to 10:00 is 2 minutes. Then, counting back from 10:00 back to 9:12 is an additional 48 minutes, making the total elapsed time 50 minutes.
2	C	Subtract the beginning time from the ending time; 7:35 back to 7:11 is 24 minutes.
3	D	Subtract the time Tanya began walking from the time she arrived home; 3:56 back to 3:31 is 25 minutes.
4	B	From 4:00 to 5:00 is one hour of elapsed time. From 5:00 until 5:27 is an additional 27 minutes, for a total elapsed time of 1 hour and 27 minutes.
5	C	From 6:12 to 7:12 is 1 hour of elapsed time. From 7:12 to 7:15 is an additional 3 minutes, for a total elapsed time of 1 hour and 3 minutes.
6	D	From 7:06 to 8:06 is one hour of elapsed time. From 8:06 to 8:13 is an additional 7 minutes, for a total elapsed time of 1 hour and 7 minutes.
7	B	From 3:11 to 4:11 is one hour of elapsed time. From 4:11 to 4:37 is an additional 26 minutes, for a total elapsed time of 1 hour and 26 minutes.
8	A	Counting back from 9:03 to 9:00 is 3 minutes. Then, counting back from 9:00 to 8:19 is an additional 41 minutes, for a total elapsed time of 44 minutes.
9	A	Subtract the beginning time from the ending time; 4:32 back to 4:17 is 15 minutes.
10	D	Counting back from 4:11 to 4:00 is 11 minutes. Then, counting back from 4:00 to 3:28 is an additional 32 minutes, for a total elapsed time of 43 minutes.
11	B	Subtract the present time from the time he has to leave; 1:30 - 1:11 = 19 minutes
12	A	From 10:45 to 11:00 is 15 minutes of elapsed time. From 11:00 to 11:25 is an additional 25 minutes, for a total elapsed time of 40 minutes.
13	A	Counting back from noon (12:00) to 11:30 is 30 minutes. Then, counting back from 11:30 to 11:29 is an additional minute, for a total elapsed time of 31 minutes.
14	A	Clock A shows 12:01 and Clock B shows 1:03. The elapsed time from 12:01 to 1:03 is 1 hour and 2 minutes.
15	D	Clock A shows 7:15 and Clock B shows 7:47. The elapsed time from 7:15 to 7:47 is 32 minutes.

Question No.	Answer	Detailed Explanation

16

	9:05	**10:55**	**12:15**
History 10:10	○	●	○
Math 8:20	●	○	○
Gym 11:30	○	○	●

In order to find the end time, add 45 minutes to the start time. Time is measured in 60 minute intervals. If the total exceeds 60 then add time to the next hour. To add 45 minutes to 8:20, add 40 minutes which will reach 9:00. Then add the remaining 5 minutes. The end time will be 9:05. Using the same strategy, 10:10 plus 45 minutes will be 10:55 and 11:30 plus 45 minutes will be 12:15.

17

Driving Start Time	**Break Time**
1:00	2:00
2:15	**3:15**
3:30	4:30
4:45	**5:45**

The correct answers are 3:15, 4:45 and 5:45. To find the break time, add one hour to the start time. Time is measured in 60 minute intervals. If the total exceeds 60 then add time to the next hour. To find the next start time after the break, add 15 minutes to the break time.

18 — C & D

Time is measured in 60 minute intervals. 60 minutes is 1 hour. The time is 4 o'clock in the first picture. The time is 6 o'clock in the second picture. 2 hours have elapsed. 2 hours can also be seen as 120 minutes since 60+60=120

19 — 30 minutes

The time is 1 o'clock in the first picture. The time is 1:30 the second picture. 30 minutes have elapsed.

20 — B

We have to subtract the time Tim left home from the time he returned; 3:45 PM - 11:30 AM. From 11:30 AM to 12 noon is 30 minutes of elapsed time. From 12 noon to 3:00 PM is 3 hours of elapsed time. From 3:00 PM to 3:45 PM is 45 minutes of elapsed time. Therefore, total elapsed time = 30 minutes + 3 hours + 45 minutes = 3 hours and 75 minutes. 3 hours and 75 minutes = 4 hours and 15 minutes.

Liquid Volume & Mass

Question No.	Answer	Detailed Explanation
1	D	The word "pound" after the number 40 indicates that 40 is a measurement of weight.
2	B	Kilograms are used to measure the mass of large, solid objects such as a table.
3	A	The amount of a liquid is also called its volume. Option C and D are not used to measure volume. Option B would be too large to measure water in a small bowl. Option A is the only logical choice.
4	B	Options A and C would not be used to measure weight. Option D would be too small to measure the weight of a table. Option B is the most logical choice.
5	A	Capacity is another word for volume. Options B, C, and D would not be used to measure volume. Option A is the most logical choice.
6	C	Option A is a measure for volume. Option B is a measure of distance or length. Option D is a measure of temperature. Option C is the most logical choice.
7	A	A gallon is a unit used to measure the volume of large amounts of liquid, whereas the other units measure smaller amounts of liquids.
8	C	Options A and B would be too light to be the weight of a typical 8-year-old, While Option D would be too heavy. Option C is the most logical choice.
9	A	Volume is a measurement associated with 3-dimensional figures. As a result, it is represented in cubic units. Volume is a measure of how many identical cubes (or parts of identical cubes) could fit within a solid figure.
10	B	Options C and D are not used to measure weight. Option A would be used to measure the weight of very large objects. Option B is the most logical choice.
11	C	Option D is not used to measure volume. Options A and B are both used to measure small amounts of liquids. Option C is the most logical choice for the large amount of water that takes up a swimming pool.
12	D	Options A, B, and C are all used to measure shorter lengths. Option D is the most logical choice.
13	A	Option C is not used to measure mass or volume. A cupcake recipe would have a very small amount of salt. Options B and D are both used to measure large quantities. Option A is the most logical choice for the small amount of salt that would be in Cupcakes.

Question No.	Answer	Detailed Explanation
14	A	Options B, C, and D are all used to measure shorter lengths and distances. Option A is used to measure large distances.
15	C	A millimeter is a very small unit of length (approximately the thickness of a fingernail).
16	Quarts & Liters	From the given options, quarts and liters are the only units used to measure liquids.
17	2 cups	The top measuring line of the cup is marked at 2 cups. This is the maximum amount of liquid it can hold. A measuring cup is a tool that can be used to measure quantities of liquid.
18	Teaspoon	From the given options, Teaspoon is the only tool used to measure small amounts of substances such as sugar.
19		This is a two-step problem. First, we calculate the total amount of water in the 8 coolers by multiplying the number of coolers (8) by the capacity of each water cooler (7 liters); 8 x 7 = 56 liters. Next, we calculate the amount of water consumed by subtracting the amount of water remained from the total amount of water; 56 - 5 = 51 liters.

Lesson 4: Graphs

Question No.	Answer	Detailed Explanation
1	B	The chart shows 3 sets of 5 tallies for Mrs. B's class in the "yes" column. Multiplying 3 x 5 the tallies represent 15 kids.
2	C	The number 14 in the "yes" column for Mrs. A's class represents 14 votes.
3	D	The "Total" row displays the overall number of votes. There is a total of 41 votes represented in the "No" column.
4	C	First, add the totals number of students who chose Science and Math. 3 + 4 = 7. The chart states that each object stands for 2 votes. Multiply the Science and Math total by 2. 7 x 2 = 14.
5	C	The tallest bar indicates the food that was chosen most often. That would be considered the "favorite."
6	D	The foods with the shortest bars represent the foods that were least liked by the kids. Both salads and wraps had the least amount of votes.
7	C	Locate "pasta" on the bottom of the graph. The bar for pasta reaches up to the 40 line.
8	B	First find the values for both fries and pizza by locating them on the x-axis and then moving over to the y-axis to see their value. Subtract the number of kids who chose pizza from the number of kids who chose fries. 50 - 40 = 10.
9	B	The title of the graph is located above the graph.
10	A	Option B is false because the graph makes no mention of amount of rain. Option C is false because the title of the graph states "rainy days" and not temperature. Option D is false because the graph only shows 5 months which is not equivalent to a year. Option A is the only choice that is true.
11	B	According to the graph, January had 2 rainy days, February had 8 rainy days, March had 4 rainy days, and April had 6 rainy days. February had the most rainy days.
12	B	Add up all the tallies to obtain the total. 6 + 4 + 8 + 4 + 3 = 25.
13	C	Subtract the number of students who chose hockey from the number of students who chose soccer. 6 - 4 = 2.
14	B	There are 8 tally marks in the baseball section. This represents the 8 students who voted for baseball as their favorite sport.
15	D	Hockey and tennis both have 4 tallies on the chart.

Question No.	Answer	Detailed Explanation

16

	5	2	4
Total votes for Friday	●	○	○
Total votes for Wednesday	○	○	●
Total votes for Monday	○	●	○

Each figure in the graph represents 1 student. 5 students voted for Friday, 4 students voted for Wednesday, and 2 students voted for Monday.

17

Type of Bat	Number of Bats Needed
Wood	4
Aluminum	4
Plastic	3

Coach Dennis needs 4 wooden bats, 4 aluminum bats, and 3 plastic bats. "Half of the bats" means that 8 bats will need to be divided in half or by 2. 8 divided by 2 equals four.

18 — A & D — Each flower on the graph represents 2 flowers. There are 8 Hibiscus flowers, 14 Rose flowers, and 6 Iris flowers.

19 — Every fifth mark is drawn across the previous four marks.

In the tally of penny coins, there are four 5s (making it 4 x 5 = 20) and two singles (2 x 1 = 2). So, there are 22 pennies. Similarly, we can find that there are 18 nickels, 14 dimes and 16 quarters.

Coins in John's Piggy Bank		
Coin	Tally	Number of Coins
Penny	ЖН ЖН ЖН ЖН II	22
Nickel	ЖН ЖН ЖН III	18
Dime	ЖН ЖН IIII	14
Quarter	ЖН ЖН ЖН I	16

Question No.	Answer	Detailed Explanation

Tally chart is used to draw the bar graph given below.

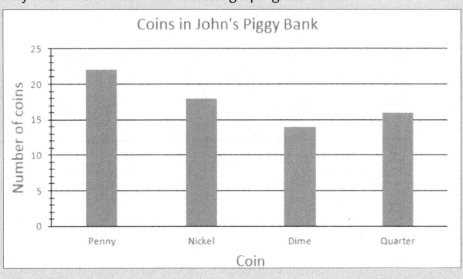

20		The left side of the Venn diagram shows the number of people who own only cats. This is 2 people

The right side shows the number of people who own only dogs which is 3 people. The center overlapping portion shows the number of people who own both cat and dog which is 2.

We need number of people who own only cat / the number of people who own only dogs which is $\frac{2}{3}$. |

Lesson 5: Measuring Length

Question No.	Answer	Detailed Explanation
1	C	Options A, B, and D are all customary units. Option C is the only metric unit.
2	B	A meter is just slightly longer than a yard. That is why a meterstick and a yardstick are almost the same length. 1 yard = 36 inches. 1 meter ≈ 39 inches.
3	C	Decimeters and centimeters are both too small to measure a table. Kilometers are used to measure long distances or lengths. Option C is the most appropriate.
4	C	Kilometers and meters are used to measure longer lengths. Grams are used to measure mass. Option C is the most appropriate.
5	A	Feet, yards, and miles are all used to measure longer lengths. The length of a pencil would be measured in inches.
6	A	Options B, C, and D are all too long to be the measure of a football. Option A is the most appropriate.
7	B	Option A and C are both too small for a football field. Option D is inappropriate because a football field is measurable. Option B is the most appropriate answer.
8	D	The width of a finger is small. Options A and B would both be too large. Option C is too small and would be more appropriate for the thickness of a fingernail. Option D is the most appropriate.
9	B	Hours are used to measure time. Yards are too small to measure a distance between two cities. Square inches are a measure of area, not distance. Option B is the most appropriate.
10	C	There are 2.54 centimeters in an inch. To convert centimeters to inches, divide 25 ÷ 2.54 = 9.84, rounding 9.84 to 10.
11	B	This ruler measures in inches. The end of the object stops at the number 8 so this object must be 8 inches.
12	C	This ruler measures in inches. The end of the object stops at the number 3 so this object must be 3 inches.
13	A	This ruler measures in inches. The end of the object stops at the number 6 so this object must be 6 inches.
14	B	Option A is false because inches are a smaller measurement unit than miles. Option C is false because a foot is longer than an inch. Option D is false because a mile is larger than a foot. Option B is the only statement that is true.
15	C	There are exactly 12 inches in one foot.

| 16 | C & D | A ruler is a tool used to measure objects in inches. A ruler is usually no more than 12 inches long. From the answer choices, a carrot and a crayon can be measured with a ruler. |
| 17 | 4 Inches | The length of the pencil is 4 inches according to the ruler. A ruler is a tool used to measure length. |

18

Measurement in inches	Measurement in half inches	Measurement in quarter inches
$2\frac{1}{2}$ inches	**5 half inches**	**10 quarter inches**
$5\frac{1}{2}$ inches	11 half inches	**22 quarter inches**
$6\frac{1}{2}$ inches	**13 half inches**	26 quarter inches

(1) 1 inch = 2 half inches; $2\frac{1}{2}$ inches = 2 inches + $\frac{1}{2}$ inch = 2 x 2 half inches + 1 half inch = 4 half inches + 1 half inch = 5 half inches.

1 half inch = 2 quarter inches. $2\frac{1}{2}$ inches = 5 half inches = 5 x 2 quarter inches = 10 quarter inches.

(2) 11 half inches = 10 half inches + 1 half inch = (10 ÷ 2) inches + $\frac{1}{2}$ inch = 5 inches + $\frac{1}{2}$ inch = $5\frac{1}{2}$ inches.

11 half inches = 11 x 2 quarter inches = 22 quarter inches.

(3) 26 quarter inches = 26 ÷ 2 half inches = 13 half inches.
13 half inches = 12 half inches + 1 half inch = (12 ÷ 2) inches + $\frac{1}{2}$ inch = 6 inches + $\frac{1}{2}$ inch = $6\frac{1}{2}$ inches.

Area

Question No.	Answer	Detailed Explanation
1	C	Area is a 2-dimensional attribute, so it must be represented in square units. Area is a measure of how many identical squares (or parts of identical squares) would be needed to cover a figure.
2	D	A postage stamp is a rectangle measuring about 1 inch on each side. Therefore, the area of a postage stamp is about 1 square inch. The other objects are all too large to measure 1 square inch as this is a very small measurement.
3	A	Area of a rectangle is calculated by multiplying length by width: 12 inches x 20 inches = 240 square inches.
4	C	If each box is a square unit, count the number of shaded boxes to get the area of the shaded region. There are 11 shaded boxes so the area is equal to 11 square units.
5	D	If each box is a square unit, count the number of boxes to get the area. There are 16 boxes so the area is equal to 16 square units.
6	C	If each box is a square unit, count the number of boxes to get the area. There are 24 boxes so the area is equal to 24 square units.
7	B	If each box is a square unit, count the number of shaded boxes to get the area of the shaded region. There are 10 shaded boxes so the area is equal to 10 square units.
8	B	If each box is a square unit, count the number of shaded boxes to get the area of the shaded region. There are 12 shaded boxes so the area is equal to 12 square units.
9	D	If each box is a square unit, count the number of shaded boxes to get the area of the shaded region. There are 9 shaded boxes so the area is equal to 9 square units.
10	D	Area of a rectangle = length x width. In this problem, we know the area and the length of the room. Let the width be w. 72 = 8 x w. What is the number when multiplied by 8 gives 72? It is 9. Therefore, w = 9 ft.

Question No.	Answer	Detailed Explanation
11		

	Yes	No
Window panes	✓	
A ball		✓
Bathroom tile	✓	
A banana		✓

Question No.	Answer	Detailed Explanation
12	4; 8; 7	**Figure A** **Figure B** **Figure C** The correct answers are 4, 8, and 7. Each shaded box is one square unit. Figure A has 4 square units shaded. Figure B has 8 square units shaded. Figure C has 7 square units shaded.
13	54 square feet	To find the area of a rectangle, multiply length by width. 6 feet x 9 feet= 54 square feet.
14	A & B	Each box is one square unit. Count the total number of square units in order to find the area. Another method is to count the square units along the width and multiply the total by the number of square units along the length.
15	B	Area of the square B is one third the area of the rectangle A. It means, we have to divide the area of the rectangle A by 3 to get the area of the square B. Area of the square B = 75 ÷ 3 = 25 sq. cm. Area of a square = side length x side length. Area of the square B = 25 sq. cm. What is the number when multiplied by itself will give 25? It is 5. Therefore, side length = 5 cm.

Relating Area to Addition & Multiplication

Question No.	Answer	Detailed Explanation
1	A	Area is calculated by multiplying length by width: 3 feet x 29 feet = 87 square feet. (Note: 3 x 29 = 29 + 29 + 29 = 87)
2	D	Area is calculated by multiplying length by width: 12 yards x 15 yards = 180 square yards. [Note: 15 x 12 = (15 x 10) + (15 x 2) = 150 + 30 = 180]
3	C	Area of a rectangle is calculated by multiplying length by width. To find the area of this rectangle, multiply 63 x 33.
4	B	Area of a rectangle is calculated by multiplying length by width: 5 meters x 10 meters = 50 square meters.
5	A	Area of a rectangle is calculated by multiplying length by width: 16 yards x 11 yards = 176 square yards. [Note: 16 x 11 = (16 x 10) + (16 x 1) = 160 + 16 = 176]
6	B	Area of a rectangle is calculated by multiplying length by width: 3 inches x (2 + 3) inches = 3 inches x 5 inches = 15 square inches.
7	D	Area of a rectangle is calculated by multiplying length by width: 7 feet x (2 + 1) feet = 7 feet x 3 feet = 21 square feet.
8	A	Area of a rectangle is calculated by multiplying length by width: 12 meters x (4 + 3) meters = 12 meters x 7 meters = 84 square meters.
9	D	Area of a rectangle is calculated by multiplying length by width: 5 inches x (5 + 2) inches = 5 inches x 7 inches = 35 square inches.
10	B	Area of a rectangle is calculated by multiplying length by width: 13 yards x (7 x 7) yards = 13 yards x 14 yards = 182 square yards.
11	C	The park is rectangular. The area of a rectangle is calculated by multiplying length by width: 50 feet x 20 feet = 1,000 square feet.
12	A	Area of a rectangle is calculated by multiplying length by width: 7 yards x 6 yards = 42 square yards.
13	C	Area of a rectangle is calculated by multiplying length by width: 30 feet x 20 feet = 600 square feet.
14	C	The area of one wall is calculated by multiplying length by width: 20 feet x 10 feet = 200 square feet. There are four identical walls, so multiply 4 by 200 to calculate the total area: 4 x 200 square feet = 800 square feet.
15	C	Area is calculated by multiplying length by width: 2 meters x 4 meters = 8 square meters.

Perimeter

Question No.	Answer	Detailed Explanation
1	C	The perimeter of a shape is the distance around the shape.
2	B	A plane figure is a two-dimensional (flat) shape. Area and perimeter are both associated with these types of objects. Volume and weight apply to 3-dimensional figures.
3	A	To find the perimeter of a rectangle, total the lengths of its four sides. 4 + 1 + 4 + 1 = 10 units
4	B	To find the perimeter of a rectangle, total the lengths of its four sides. 1 + 2 + 1 + 2 = 6 units
5	A	To find the perimeter of the shaded area, count the edges that surround the outside of the shaded area. There are 16 sides around the shaded area so the perimeter is 16.
6	C	A rhombus has 4 equal sides and the perimeter is equal to the sum of those 4 sides. To calculate the length of each side, divide the perimeter by 4. 20 ÷ 4 = 5.
7	B	Because a rhombus has four equal sides, to find its perimeter multiply the length of one of its sides by four. 3 x 4 = 12 centimeters
8	C	A square has 4 equal sides and the perimeter is equal to the sum of those 4 sides. To calculate the length of each side, divide the perimeter by 4. 80 ÷ 4 = 20.
9	A	To find the perimeter of the figure, count the edges that surround the outside of the figure. There are 20 sides around the figure so the perimeter is 20.
10	B	The yard is rectangular. To find its perimeter, total the lengths of its four sides. 30 + 15 + 30 + 15 = 90 feet
11	A	To find the perimeter of the figure, count the edges that surround the outside of the figure. There are 20 sides around the figure so the perimeter is 20.
12	C	The field is rectangular. To find its perimeter, add the lengths of its four sides. 23 + 32 + 23 + 32 = 110 yards
13	A	To find the perimeter of a rectangle, total the lengths of its four sides. 15 + 12 + 15 + 12 = 54 feet
14	D	To find the perimeter of a rectangle, total the lengths of its four sides. 16 + 11 + 16 + 11 = 54 feet

Question No.	Answer	Detailed Explanation
15	D	To find the perimeter of the shaded area, count the edges that surround the outside of the shaded area. There are 16 sides around the shaded area so the perimeter is 16.
16	D	To find the perimeter of a rectangle, total the lengths of its four sides. 3 + 29 + 3 + 29 = 64 feet
17	C	The park is rectangular. To find its perimeter, total the lengths of its four sides. 20 + 50 + 20 + 50 = 140 feet
18	B	To find the perimeter of a rectangle, total the lengths of its four sides. 33 + 53 + 33 + 53 = 172 inches
19	C	To find the perimeter of a rectangle, total the lengths of its four sides. 10 + 5 + 10 + 5 = 30 meters
20	A	To solve for the missing side, plug in what you know into the formula for perimeter: 2W + 2L = P (2 x 3) + 2x = 16 To solve for x: 2x = 16 - 6 = 10. Divide 10 by 2 to find one side; x = 5 feet.
21	A	To solve for the missing side, plug in what you know into the formula for perimeter: 2W + 2L = P (2 x 7) + 2x = 20 To solve for x: 2x = 20 - 14 = 6 Divide 6 by 2 to find one side; x = 3 feet.
22	D	If there are 4 sides to the rectangular park, the measurements of each side would be 20, 50, 20, 50. The question asks for the least amount of fencing needed for 3 sides. They should choose to fence the two 20-foot sides and one of the 50-foot sides. The amount of fencing material needed would be 20 + 20 + 50 = 90 feet.
23	C	To solve for the missing side, plug in what you know into the formula for perimeter: 2W + 2L = P. (2 x 12) + 2x = 38, now solve for x. To solve for x: x = (38 - 24) ÷ 2, x = 7.
24	B	To solve for the missing side, plug in what you know into the formula for perimeter: 2W + 2L = P (2 x 5) + 2x = 24 To solve for x : 2x = 24 - 10 = 14 Divide 14 by 2 to find one side; x = 7 inches.

84

LumosLearning.com

Question No.	Answer	Detailed Explanation
25	B	To solve for the missing side, plug in what you know into the formula for perimeter: 2W + 2L = P (2 x 13) + 2x = 54 To solve for x: 2x = 54 - 26 = 28 Divide 28 by 2 to find one side; x = 14 yards.
26	A & D	The perimeter is the distance around the outside of a plane figure. The perimeter can be found by adding the length of a figure's sides.
27	18 units	The perimeter can be found by adding the length of a figure's sides. 3 + 3 + 6 + 6= 18.
28	2 cm	A rhombus has 4 equal sides. Perimeter can be found by adding the length of a figure's sides. Perimeter of the figure is 8 cm. Rhombus with four 2 cm sides is the only figure that has a perimeter of 8 cm., because 2 + 2 + 2 + 2 = 8 cm.
29		A regular hexagon has six equal sides. Therefore, perimeter of the hexagon = 6 x length of one side = 6 x 8 = 48 cm. A regular octagon has eight equal sides. Therefore, perimeter of the octagon = 8 x length of one side = 8 x 7 = 56 cm. 56 cm > 48 cm. Therefore, perimeter of the octagon > perimeter of the hexagon

Question Answer No.		Detailed Explanation		

30

	15 sq. cm.	10 sq. cm.	12 sq. cm.
Perimeter = 16 cm	✓		✓
Perimeter = 14 cm		✓	✓
Perimeter = 22 cm		✓	

Let L be the length of the rectangle and W be the width of the rectangle. Perimeter = 2 (L + W)

(1) Perimeter = 16; 2 x (L + W) = 16; L + W = 16 ÷ 2 = 8. We have to find the length and the width of the rectangle whose sum is 8 cm, and then find the area. Find the areas of the rectangles by substituting L = 1, 2, 3 etc. Among the choices given, there are 2 possible areas. (a) If L = 2, W = 8 - 2 = 6 . Area = L x W = 2 x 6 = 12 sq. cm. (b) If L = 3, W = 8 - 3 = 5. Area = 3 x 5 = 15 sq. cm.

(2) Perimeter = 14; 2 x (L + W) = 14; L + W = 14 ÷ 2 = 7. We have to find the length and the width of the rectangle whose sum is 7 cm, and then find the area. Find the areas of the rectangles by substituting L = 1, 2, 3 etc. Among the choices given, there are 2 possible areas. (a) If L = 2, W = 7 - 2 = 5. Area = 2 x 5 = 10 sq. cm. (b) If L = 3, W = 7 - 3 = 4. Area = 3 x 4 = 12 sq. cm.

(3) Perimeter = 22; 2 x (L + W) = 22; L + W = 22 ÷ 2 = 11. We have to find the length and the width of the rectangle whose sum is 11 cm, and then find the area. Find the areas of the rectangles by substituting L = 1, 2, 3 etc. Among the choices given, there is only one possibility. If L = 1, W = 11 - 1 = 10. Area = 1 x 10 = 10 sq. cm.

Geometry

2-Dimensional Shapes

1. **Fill in the blank with the correct term.**
   Closed, plane figures that have straight sides are called _____ .

   Ⓐ parallelograms
   Ⓑ line segments
   Ⓒ polygons
   Ⓓ squares

2. **Which of the following shapes is not a polygon?**

   Ⓐ Square
   Ⓑ Hexagon
   Ⓒ Circle
   Ⓓ Pentagon

3. **Complete this statement.**
   A rectangle must have _____ .

   Ⓐ four right angles
   Ⓑ four straight angles
   Ⓒ four obtuse angles
   Ⓓ four acute angles

4. **How many sides does a trapezoid have?**

   Ⓐ 4
   Ⓑ 8
   Ⓒ 6
   Ⓓ 10

5. **Complete the following statement.**
   A square is always a _____ .

   Ⓐ rhombus
   Ⓑ parallelogram
   Ⓒ rectangle
   Ⓓ All of the above

6. Which of these statements is true?

   Ⓐ A square and a triangle have the same number of angles.
   Ⓑ A triangle has more angles than a square.
   Ⓒ A square has more angles than a triangle.
   Ⓓ A square and a triangle each have no angles.

7. Which of these statements is true?

   Ⓐ A rectangle has more sides than a trapezoid.
   Ⓑ A parallelogram and a trapezoid have the same number of sides.
   Ⓒ A triangle has more sides than a trapezoid.
   Ⓓ A triangle has more sides than a square.

8. Complete this statement.
   A trapezoid must have _____.

   Ⓐ two acute angles
   Ⓑ two right angles
   Ⓒ one pair of parallel sides
   Ⓓ two pairs of parallel sides

9. Complete the following statement.
   Squares, rectangles, rhombi and trapezoids are all _____.

   Ⓐ triangles
   Ⓑ quadrilaterals
   Ⓒ angles
   Ⓓ round

10. Which of these shapes is a quadrilateral?

   Ⓐ circle
   Ⓑ triangle
   Ⓒ rectangle
   Ⓓ pentagon

11. Which of these shapes is NOT a quadrilateral?

   Ⓐ square
   Ⓑ trapezoid
   Ⓒ rectangle
   Ⓓ triangle

12. Name the figure shown below.

Ⓐ Trapezoid
Ⓑ Square
Ⓒ Pentagon
Ⓓ Rhombus

13. Name the object shown below.

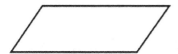

Ⓐ Rectangle
Ⓑ Parallelogram
Ⓒ Trapezoid
Ⓓ Rhombus

14. The figure shown below is a _____ .

Ⓐ parallelogram
Ⓑ rectangle
Ⓒ quadrilateral
Ⓓ All of the above

Name: _____   Date: _____

15. The figure below is a _____ .

Ⓐ triangle
Ⓑ square
Ⓒ rhombus
Ⓓ trapezoid

16. Are these figures quadrilaterals? Select yes or no.

	Yes	No
Circle		
Star		
Square		
Rectangle		

17. Circle the parallelogram.

  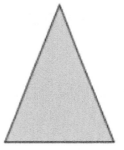

18. For each polygon in the first column, an attribute is defined in the second column. Write true, if the polygon has the mentioned attribute or write false if the polygon does not have the mentioned attribute.

Polygon	Attribute	True or False
Rhombus	It has two sets of parallel sides	True
Parallelogram	All the angles are equal	
Rectangle	Opposite sides are equal	

19. Draw a quadrilateral which has three obtuse angles.

Instruction : An obtuse angle is an angle which measures more than 90° but less than 180°.

20. Which of the following figures have at least one set parallel sides? Note that more than one option may be correct.

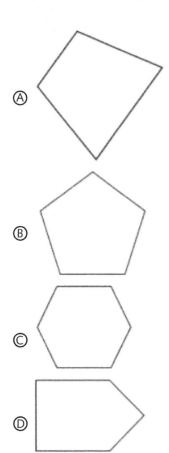

Ⓐ

Ⓑ

Ⓒ

Ⓓ

Online Resources: 2-Dimensional Shapes

URL	QR Code
http://lumoslearning.com/a/m13445	

 Videos   Apps   Sample Questions

93

NOTES

Shape Partitions

1. **What is the dotted line that divides a shape into two equal parts called?**

    Ⓐ a middle line
    Ⓑ a line of symmetry
    Ⓒ a line of congruency
    Ⓓ a divider

2. **A square has how many lines of symmetry?**

    Ⓐ 8
    Ⓑ 4
    Ⓒ 1
    Ⓓ 2

3. **Which of the following has NO lines of symmetry?**

4. **Which of the following objects has more than one line of symmetry?**

 Ⓐ

 Ⓑ

 Ⓒ

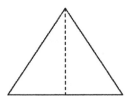 Ⓓ

5. **What fraction of this triangle is shaded?**

Ⓐ $\frac{1}{2}$

Ⓑ $\frac{2}{2}$

Ⓒ $\frac{0}{2}$

Ⓓ $\frac{3}{4}$

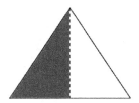
6. **What fraction of this triangle is shaded?**

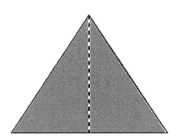

Ⓐ $\frac{0}{2}$

Ⓑ $\frac{1}{2}$

Ⓒ $\frac{2}{2}$

Ⓓ $\frac{3}{4}$

7. **What fraction of this triangle is shaded?**

Ⓐ $\frac{0}{2}$

Ⓑ $\frac{1}{2}$

Ⓒ $\frac{2}{2}$

Ⓓ $\frac{3}{4}$

8. **What fraction of this square is shaded?**

Ⓐ $\dfrac{0}{2}$

Ⓑ $\dfrac{1}{2}$

Ⓒ $\dfrac{2}{2}$

Ⓓ $\dfrac{3}{4}$

9. **What fraction of this square is shaded?**

Ⓐ $\dfrac{0}{4}$

Ⓑ $\dfrac{1}{4}$

Ⓒ $\dfrac{2}{4}$

Ⓓ $\dfrac{1}{2}$

10. What fraction of this square is shaded?

Ⓐ $\dfrac{0}{4}$

Ⓑ $\dfrac{1}{4}$

Ⓒ $\dfrac{1}{2}$

Ⓓ $\dfrac{3}{4}$

11. What fraction of this rectangle is shaded?

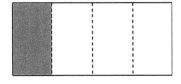

Ⓐ $\dfrac{0}{4}$

Ⓑ $\dfrac{1}{4}$

Ⓒ $\dfrac{2}{4}$

Ⓓ $\dfrac{3}{4}$

12. What fraction of this circle is shaded?

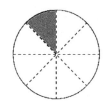

Ⓐ $\dfrac{1}{8}$

Ⓑ $\dfrac{1}{4}$

Ⓒ $\dfrac{1}{2}$

Ⓓ $\dfrac{3}{4}$

13. What fraction of this circle is shaded?

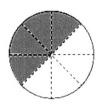

Ⓐ $\dfrac{1}{8}$

Ⓑ $\dfrac{1}{4}$

Ⓒ $\dfrac{5}{8}$

Ⓓ $\dfrac{4}{8}$

14. The area of the entire rectangle shown below is 48 square feet. What is the area of the shaded portion?

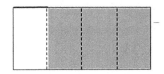

Ⓐ 36 square feet
Ⓑ 48 square feet
Ⓒ 144 square feet
Ⓓ 12 square feet

15. If the area of the entire rectangle below is 36 square feet. What is the area of the shaded portion?

Ⓐ 8 square feet
Ⓑ 9 square feet
Ⓒ 144 square feet
Ⓓ 12 square feet

16. Do these figures have a line of symmetry? Select yes or no.

	Yes	No

17. Circle the shape that has a line of symmetry.

18. If the area of the whole rectangle is 28, what is the area of the shaded portion? Write your answer in the box given below.

19. Shade one third of the figure below.

20. A circle has an area of 96 sq. cm. The circle is divided into 8 equal parts. Which of the following statements are correct? Select all the correct answers.

Ⓐ If you shade 3 parts, the area of the shaded portion is 32 sq. cm.
Ⓑ If you shade 4 parts, the area of the shaded portion is 48 sq. cm.
Ⓒ If you shade 7 parts, the area of the shaded portion is 84 sq. cm.
Ⓓ If you shade 2 parts, the area of the shaded portion is 24 sq. cm.

Online Resources: Shape Partitions

URL	QR Code
http://lumoslearning.com/a/m13446	

 Videos   Apps   Sample Questions

End of Geometry

103

NOTES

Answer Key

and

Detailed Explanations

2-Dimensional Shapes

Question No.	Answer	Detailed Explanation
1	C	By definition, a polygon is a plane (flat), closed figure with only straight sides.
2	C	A polygon must have only straight sides. A circle is the only option that does not fit this criteria. Since it is curved.
3	A	A rectangle is a quadrilateral (4-sided polygon) with 4 right angles.
4	A	A trapezoid is a quadrilateral which means it has 4 sides.
5	D	A square is a rhombus parallelogram, and rectangle because all of these figures are four-sided and contain two sets of parallel sides.
6	C.	Answer C is true because a square has 4 angles and a triangle has 3 angles.
7	B	Answer B is true because a parallelogram and a trapezoid both have 4 sides.
8	C	A trapezoid is a quadrilateral with one pair of parallel sides.
9	B	A quadrilateral is a figure with four straight sides and four angles. Squares, rectangles, rhombi, and trapezoids all have 4 sides.
10	C	A quadrilateral is a figure with four straight sides and four angles. A rectangle fits this description, where as a triangle has 3 sides, a circle is round, and a pentagon has 5 sides.
11	D	A quadrilateral is a figure with four straight sides and four angles. A triangle is the only choice that does not fit this description. Since it has only 3 sides.
12.	A	A trapezoid is a quadrilateral that contains only one pair of parallel sides.
13	B	A parallelogram is a quadrilateral with two pairs of opposite parallel sides. The figure is not a rectangle because it does not have right angles. It is not a rhombus because the sides are not all equal in length. It is not a trapezoid because a trapezoid only has one set of parallel sides.
14	D	The shape is a parallelogram because it has two pairs of parallel sides. It is a quadrilateral because it has 4 sides. It is a rectangle because it is a parallelogram with all right angles.
15	C	A rhombus is a quadrilateral with 4 equal sides. This figure is not a square because it does not have right angles. Triangles are three-sided, while trapezoids do not have four equal sides.

16

	Yes	No
Circle		✓
Star		✓
Square	✓	
Rectangle	✓	

A quadrilateral is a four-sided polygon with four angles. Squares and rectangles belong in this category. Circles and stars are not quadrilaterals.

17

A parallelogram is a (non-self-intersecting) quadrilateral with two pairs of parallel sides. Ovals and triangles are not parallelograms.

18

Polygon	Attribute	True or False
Rhombus	It has two sets of parallel sides	True
Parallelogram	All the angles are equal	**False**
Rectangle	Opposite sides are equal	**True**

In a parallelogram, opposite angles are equal. Adjacent angles need not be equal.

A rectangle is a special type of parallelogram, whose angles measure 90o each. Since a rectangle is a type of parallelogram, it has the attribute: opposite sides are equal.

19

In the above quadrilateral, angles ADC, DAB and ABC are obtuse angles.

20 — **C & D**

The first figure is a trapezoid. It has one pair of parallel sides. The second figure is a pentagon. It has no parallel sides. The third figure is a regular hexagon. It has 3 sets of parallel sides. The fourth figure has one set of parallel sides.

Shape Partitions

Question No.	Answer	Detailed Explanation
1	B	A line of symmetry is an imaginary line that divides an object into two mirror images.
2	B	A line of symmetry is an imaginary line that divides an object into two mirror images. A square can be divided across the length, across the width, down diagonally from left to right, and down diagonally from right to left.
3	C	A line of symmetry is an imaginary line that divides an object into two mirror images. Answer C cannot be divided in such a way.
4	A	A line of symmetry is an imaginary line that divides an object into two mirror images. The object in Answer A can have a line of symmetry at multiple points, for example across the length, across the width, and diagonally.
5	C	No parts of the triangle are shaded yet the shape is divided into two parts. To form a fraction, the numerator is the part and the denominator is the whole. Since no parts are shaded, the numerator would be 0.
6	B	One part of the triangle is shaded yet the shape is divided into two parts. To form a fraction, the numerator is the part and the denominator is the whole.
7	C	Two parts of the triangle are shaded and the shape is divided into two parts. To form a fraction, the numerator is the part and the denominator is the whole.
8	B	One part of the square is shaded and the shape is divided into two parts. To form a fraction, the numerator is the part and the denominator is the whole.
9	B	One part of the square is shaded and the shape is divided into four parts. To form a fraction, the numerator is the part and the denominator is the whole.
10	D	Three parts of the square are shaded and the shape is divided into four parts. To form a fraction, the numerator is the part and the denominator is the whole.

Question No.	Answer	Detailed Explanation
11	B	One part of the rectangle is shaded yet the shape is divided into four parts. To form a fraction, the numerator is the parts and the denominator is the whole.
12	A	One part of the circle is shaded yet the shape is divided into eight parts. To form a fraction, the numerator is the parts and the denominator is the whole.
13	D	Four parts of the circle are shaded yet the shape is divided into eight parts. To form a fraction, the numerator is the parts and the denominator is the whole.
14	A	The shape is divided into four equal parts. This means that each part has the same area. If the total area is known, divide this area by 4 to calculate the area of each part. $48 \div 4 = 12$. Since one part is left unshaded, subtract 12 from the total area of 48 to find that the shaded portion represents 36 square feet.
15	B	The shape is divided into four equal parts. This means that each part has the same area. If the total area is known, divide this area by 4 to calculate the area of each part. $36 \div 4 = 9$. Each piece has an area of 9 square feet. The problem asks for the area of the shaded portion. There is only one shaded section, so the area equals 9 square feet.
16		

	Yes	No
♥		
▽		
◴		

A figure that can reflect over a line and appear unchanged has reflection symmetry or line symmetry. All 3 figures have a line of symmetry.

Question No.	Answer	Detailed Explanation
17	Star	A figure that can reflect over a line and appear unchanged has reflection symmetry or line symmetry. The star has a line of symmetry.
18	14	The shapes is divided into 4 equal parts. Each part has the same area. Since the area of the whole figure is 28, divide 28 by 4. The area of each shaded part is 7. There are 2 shaded parts so add 7 + 7. The area of the shaded portion is 14.
19	4 cells	The figure is divided into 12 equal parts. One third of 12 means we have to divide 12 by 3; 12 ÷ 3 = 4. So, we have to shade 4 cells.
20	B, C & D	The circle is divided into 8 equal parts. This means that each part has the same area. Divide the total area by 8 to calculate the area of each part; 96 ÷ 8 = 12 sq. cm. Each part has an area of 12 sq. cm. (1) When we shade 3 parts, the shaded portion has an area of 3 x 12 = 36 sq. cm. Therefore, option (A) is wrong. (2) When we shade 4 parts, the shaded portion has an area of 4 x 12 = 48 sq. cm. Therefore, option (B) is correct. (3) When we shade 7 parts, the shaded portion has an area of 7 x 12 = 84 sq. cm. Therefore, option (C) is correct. (4) When we shade 2 parts, the shaded portion has an area of 2 x 12 = 24 sq. cm. Therefore, option (D) is correct.

Additional Information

What if I buy more than one Lumos Study Program?

Step 1
Visit the URL and login to your account.
http://www.lumoslearning.com

Step 2
Click on 'My tedBooks' under the "Account" tab.
Place the Book Access Code and submit.

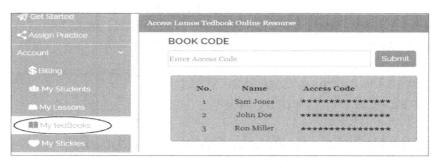

Step 3
To add the new book for a registered student, choose the
⊙ Existing Student button and select the student and submit.

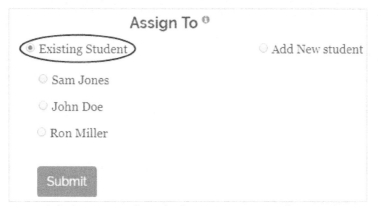

To add the new book for a new student, choose the ⊙ Add New student
button and complete the student registration.

Assign To ⊙

○ Existing Student   ◉ Add New student

Register Your TedBook

Student Name:*   Enter First Name   Enter Last Name

Student Login*

Password*

Submit

Lumos StepUp® Mobile App
FAQ For Students

What is the Lumos StepUp® App?

It is a FREE application you can download onto your Android Smartphones, tablets, iPhones, and iPads.

What are the Benefits of the StepUp® App?

This mobile application gives convenient access to Practice Tests, Common Core State Standards, Online Workbooks, and learning resources through your Smartphone and tablet computers.
- Eleven Technology enhanced question types in both MATH and ELA
- Sample questions for Arithmetic drills
- Standard specific sample questions
- Instant access to the Common Core State Standards
- Jokes and cartoons to make learning fun!

Do I Need the StepUp® App to Access Online Workbooks?

No, you can access Lumos StepUp® Online Workbooks through a personal computer. The StepUp® app simply enhances your learning experience and allows you to conveniently access StepUp® Online Workbooks and additional resources through your smart phone or tablet.

How can I Download the App?

Visit **lumoslearning.com/a/stepup-app** using your Smartphone or tablet and follow the instructions to download the app.

**QR Code
for Smartphone
Or Tablet Users**

Lumos StepUp® Mobile App FAQ
For Parents and Teachers

What is the Lumos StepUp® App?

It is a free app that teachers can use to easily access real-time student activity information as well as assign learning resources to students. Parents can also use it to easily access school-related information such as homework assigned by teachers and PTA meetings. It can be downloaded onto smart phones and tablets from popular App Stores.

What are the Benefits of the Lumos StepUp® App?

It provides convenient access to

- Standards aligned learning resources for your students
- An easy to use Dashboard
- Student progress reports
- Active and inactive students in your classroom
- Professional development information
- Educational Blogs

How can I Download the App?

Visit **lumoslearning.com/a/stepup-app** using your Smartphone or tablet and follow the instructions to download the app.

QR Code
for Smartphone
Or Tablet Users

Common Core Standards Cross-reference Table

CCSS	Standard Description	Page No.	Question No.
3.MD.A.1	Tell and write time to the nearest minute and measure time intervals in minutes. Solve word problems involving addition and subtraction of time intervals in minutes, e.g., by representing the problem on a number line diagram.	4 and 12	1 to 20 12 to 17
3.MD.A.2	Measure and estimate liquid volumes and masses of objects using standard units of grams (g), kilograms (kg), and liters (l).[1] Add, subtract, multiply, or divide to solve one-step word problems involving masses or volumes that are given in the same units, e.g., by using drawings (such as a beaker with a measurement scale) to represent the problem.	19	1 to 19
3.MD.B.3	Draw a scaled picture graph and a scaled bar graph to represent a data set with several categories. Solve one- and two-step "how many more" and "how many less" problems using information presented in scaled bar graphs. For example, draw a bar graph in which each square in the bar graph might represent 5 pets.	25	1 to 20
3.MD.B.4	Generate measurement data by measuring lengths using rulers marked with halves and fourths of an inch. Show the data by making a line plot, where the horizontal scale is marked off in appropriate units— whole numbers, halves, or quarters.	37	1 to 19
3.MD.C.5	Recognize area as an attribute of plane figures and understand concepts of area measurement.	43	1 to 15
3.MD.C.6	Measure areas by counting unit squares (square cm, square m, square in, square ft, and improvised units).		
3.MD.C.7	Relate area to the operations of multiplication and addition.	49	1 to 15
3.MD.D.8	Solve real world and mathematical problems involving perimeters of polygons, including finding the perimeter given the side lengths, finding an unknown side length, and exhibiting rectangles with the same perimeter and different areas or with the same area and different perimeters.	55	1 to 30
3.G.A.1	Understand that shapes in different categories (e.g., rhombuses, rectangles, and others) may share attributes (e.g., having four sides), and that the shared attributes can define a larger category (e.g., quadrilaterals). Recognize rhombuses, rectangles, and squares as examples of quadrilaterals, and draw examples of quadrilaterals that do not belong to any of these subcategories.	91	1 to 20

CCSS	Standard Description	Page No.	Question No.
3.G.A.2	Partition shapes into parts with equal areas. Express the area of each part as a unit fraction of the whole. For example, partition a shape into 4 parts with equal area, and describe the area of each part as 1/4 of the area of the shape.	98	1 to 20

School Supplemental Program

COMPUTER-BASED SKILLS PRACTICE AND ASSESSMENT REHEARSAL

- ➤ Standards-aligned workbooks

- ➤ Practice tests that mirror state assessments

- ➤ Fifteen tech-enhanced items practice

- ➤ Resource recommendations such as apps, books, & videos

- ➤ Personalized learning assignments for students

Call us for more information

888 - 309 - 8227

lumoslearning.com/a/online-program

Trusted by over 60,000 Students, 600 Schools, & 6000 Teachers

PARTIAL CUSTOMER LIST

MARY D. COGHILL
CHARTER SCHOOL
"Where Achievement Matters"

A. W. JAMES ELEMENTARY SCHOOL
Our Greater Is Coming

ST. MARY'S
ELEMENTARY
LANCASTER, NJ

TEANECK PUBLIC SCHOOLS

Pemberton Township Schools
Denbo/Crichton
Elementary Campus

WELCOME
Nancy Lopez Elementary

Other Books in SkillBuilder Series

Reading Comprehension SkillBuilder

- Literature
- Informational Text
- Evidence-based Reading

English Language and Grammar SkillBuilder

- Conventions
- Vocabulary
- Knowledge of Language

Operations and Algebraic Thinking SkillBuilder

- Multiplication
- Division

Fractions and Base Ten SkillBuilder

- Addition & Subtraction
- Fractions of a Whole

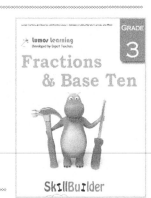

http://lumoslearning.com/a/sbtb